"In thi̶ ‎ bout
his jou ‎ licy
advoca ‎ way,
reader‎ ‎ MW01228708 ‎ ‎ can be
valuable to all who are striving to follow Christ and live in a
way that makes a difference. Richard's story reads like a
devotional book that will leave the reader considering their
own life purpose. You may not agree with everything Richard
says, but you will appreciate the kindhearted way he says it. I
gladly recommend his book to you."

TODD GRAY
Executive Director, Kentucky Baptist Convention

"The task given to the church by Jesus Christ is nothing less
than to disciple nations. It is for this purpose that Christians
are then commissioned by God to a vocational calling and to
live as godly citizens in the public square. *Christianity &
Politics* is a personal, warm, and honest account of Richard's
own journey into the realm of civic and cultural engagement.
It is a great primer for godly Christians who want guidance
about how to engage in the process of citizenship. It also
provides both a pathway and a set of principles for those who
sense a personal calling into the political and public policy
arena. *Christianity & Politics* comes with my wholehearted
endorsement!"

DARROW MILLER
Co-founder of Disciple Nations Alliance and author of
Discipling Nations: The Power of Truth to Transform Cultures

"I am thankful for the work of Richard Nelson and the Commonwealth Policy Center. Christians desperately need guidance and practical wisdom for knowing how to navigate the very challenging political and cultural currents all around us. In the state of Kentucky, we are well served by the Commonwealth Policy Center. I'm thankful for Richard Nelson and the good work he does on behalf of our state and its citizens."

ALBERT MOHLER JR.
President, The Southern Baptist Theological Seminary

"The New Testament urges us to make the teaching about God our Savior attractive (Titus 2:10). But sadly, when most Christ-followers get involved in politics, they make the teaching about God repulsive—especially to outsiders. Richard Nelson's book teaches how to stand firmly against the cultural evils of our day and be engaged in the vital issues of our time, yet be known for what we are for rather than what we are against. Relying on his years of experience, Richard helps believers to 'speak the truth in love so that in all things we will grow up to Him who is the head, that is, Christ' (Ephesians 4:15)."

BOB RUSSELL
Retired Senior Pastor, Southeast Christian
Church, Louisville, Kentucky

"I've known Richard Nelson for many years now and can testify to how the Lord has used Richard's story and his work to advance the common good through the church's mobilization. This book is not partisan hackery. It comes from a man who has the goal of seeing the good advanced. As this book attests to, all it takes to impact where the Lord has placed you is a basic commitment to get engaged and involved. If Christians and conservatives had fifty Richard Nelsons and the temperament he exudes scattered throughout the states, our nation would be better off. Take this book as a story of one man whose work can inspire others, too."

ANDREW T. WALKER
Associate Professor of Christian Ethics and Public Theology,
The Southern Baptist Theological Seminary

CHRISTIANITY & POLITICS

A MEMOIR OF SPIRITUAL FORMATION AND
FIELD GUIDE FOR CHRISTIANS IN
THE PUBLIC ARENA

RICHARD RYAN NELSON

COMMONWEALTH POLICY PRESS

Christianity & Politics: A Memoir of Spiritual Formation and Field Guide for Christians in the Public Arena

Copyright © 2024 by Richard Ryan Nelson

First printing 2024

Dewey Decimal Classification: 261.7

Subject Heading: CHRISTIANITY AND POLITICAL AFFAIRS

Cover and book design by Jennifer Stec, 511 Professional Editing Services

Library of Congress Cataloging-in-Publication Data

Nelson, Richard Ryan

Christianity & politics: a memoir of spiritual formation and field guide for christians in the public arena / Richard Ryan Nelson, 1969–

ISBN 979-8-218-46304-5 (paperback)

ISBN 979-8-218-47439-3 (e-book)

1. Christian life. 2. Political Science

LCCN 2024913312

All proceeds from the sale of this book support the work of the Commonwealth Policy Center.

CONTENTS

To Jesus Christ, my Lord and Savior. I'm forever indebted to His redeeming and sacrificial love. He is the true and rightful ruler over all creation. May He be honored in these pages, and may His people who engage in the public arena find encouragement.

ACKNOWLEDGMENTS

This book has been a labor of love and would not be possible without numerous people who poured into my life and into the work of the Commonwealth Policy Center (CPC) over the years. First, to the past and present board members who dedicated their time and talents to help this work thrive: Marty Bozarth, Brian Crall, Jeff Davis, Leighan Dickerson, Andy French, Kevin Gaunce, Rick Hardison, Paul Harrell, Jeff Hausner, Angela Minter, Brian Schuette, and Jordan Tong. Thank you for allowing me to take time off to write this.

Thank you to the CPC staff: Jenny Bennett, Cole Cuzick, Christopher Parr, Alex Richey, and Justin Warner. We could not have accomplished all the projects and made such an overall impact without your hard work. Thank you for proofreading and for your helpful comments. You've all been a joy to work with.

Special thanks to Jennifer Stec, whose outstanding editorial skills and hard work make this a much better book than when she first laid eyes on it. Thank you for going above and beyond the original task of copy editing.

To the many supporters of CPC who have sowed into this work over the years: please know that your generous support made this work possible.

To Bobby Jo, my wife and encourager, you are truly my Ruth.

INTRODUCTION

This is a story of my political journey. It's also a glimpse into my spiritual journey—one filled with detours and ironies. I'm a Northern boy who ended up in the South. I love the outdoors and intended to make environmental policy my career, but I ended up in a field of work with a very different environment and addressing very different policies. It's unlike anything I had ever envisioned.

I grew up hunting, fishing, and loving all things outdoors. I studied wildlife management and biology at the University of Wisconsin-Stevens Point (UWSP). I intended to become a wildlife manager, preferably in a place where the hunting seasons were long and the game plentiful. Unfortunately, the doors of opportunity in environmental management were closed, but the door opened for me to work for a Christian public policy organization.

I also grew up in a Christian home. We went to church every Sunday and prayed around the dinner table every evening as a family. The nondenominational church had much to say about piety and personal morality but little about culture, contemporary issues, and life's tough questions. As I grew older and more inquisitive, inadequate answers weakened my faith. By the time I got to college, what little faith I had left was displaced by the intellectual pursuits offered by college professors in my first two years as an undergrad.

During my junior year at UWSP, God put me on a path to rediscover my faith through becoming a father and being responsible for a family. I had to live according to the faith in a different context—no longer as an individual beholden to very few, but as a parent with a helpless and precious child totally dependent upon me and her mother. There are things in life one cannot fully understand until seen from a different vantage point. This is true when one enters marriage and when one becomes a parent. Through these new stations in life, the reality of God and my need for Him became evident.

I was accepted to Regent University School of Law upon graduation and, after a semester, realized that was not where my gifting and passion were. I transferred to the School of Government, where I studied public policy, hoping to one day do environmental policy. But something more important happened there. A group of mature men mentored me. They taught a Christian view of the world I had not heard before, despite the countless Sundays I sat in the pews listening to sermon after sermon. I learned that if the Bible was truly God speaking to man, it must be true in all areas of life, or it was not true at all. A challenge posed by C. S. Lewis forced me to wrestle with belief. He said, "Christianity, if false, is of no importance, and if true, of infinite importance. The only thing it cannot be is moderately important."[1] At this point of pondering life's biggest questions during grad school, God got hold of me.

I'm an introvert by nature, but my early professional career put me on a course that required engaging with all kinds of people on a regular basis. In my journey, I've discovered that I have extroverted tendencies. I like people and good conversation. However, imprinted on my DNA is a love of reading, writing, and thinking. I feel most comfortable learning, processing, and vision casting. Yet my career path catapulted me into the public realm and onto some big stages with some of the highest-level officials and celebrities. However, God's mercy and the profound change it worked in my life were more important. It's been humbling and sometimes painful, but a great privilege to see His hand at work leading to significant political changes in the Commonwealth.

This is also a memoir of sorts. It's my intention to share lessons I have learned, mainly in a political and religious context. Not all of it has been pretty. Disappointments, betrayals, and soul-crushing events have shaped me, and I am not the same man I was when I began this journey. I'm more cautious about making judgments. Grief over a broken world grips me. I'm more easily moved today by those who are suffering and more inclined to sympathize with the broken and hurting. If any good has come about through me, it is because of God's grace in my life.

I have also come to realize that while politics and public policy are important arenas and worthy pursuits, real societal change comes from spiritual awakening. Jesus Christ is truly the Savior of the world who is making all things new and will one day take His rightful place of rulership over all creation. I long to reside in that new creation, in a new body, part of a new family, with the Risen King. My hope is that this book helps you glorify the Risen King in your life and calling.

PART I

A PATH TO PUBLIC SERVICE

1

SO, YOU WANT TO RUN FOR OFFICE?

"Leader Wilkins, I'd like to run for the state House of Delegates." I sat across the desk from the Minority Leader of the Virginia House of Delegates. Behind him were solid wood paneled walls that reached the tall ceiling. Mementos from his district tastefully decorated his large office in Richmond. I told him that I wanted to run for the state House and unseat the far-left Democrat representing the Virginia Beach district I was living in.

On my way to his office, I passed a hallowed wing in the Capitol where busts of Confederate generals—Virginia's favorite sons—filled the room. Down the hall was the Chamber of the House of Delegates. In front of the Speaker's dais was a royal scepter. The building, crafted of marble and stone, demanded respect. It was an architectural feat steeped in history and filled with important people doing important things. I wanted to be a part of it.

I was in my last semester of graduate school studying public policy. A legislator I befriended set up a meeting with the Republican minority leader. "Well, son, here's what you need to do," Leader Vance Wilkins advised. "Settle into the community. Run a business. Make some money. Raise your family. And then, in about 20 years, you can run for office." It wasn't the answer my 25-year-old ears wanted to hear, but it was sound counsel. I was saddled with student loan debt and had a young family—a wife and two young children—to care for. I needed a job, preferably one in my field so I could pay the bills. My family needed me more than I needed to run for office.

I had a strong desire to make a difference and more enthusiasm and energy than I probably had sense. What I didn't realize then but understand now is that I was certainly not ready to be a good representative. I may have had an education, but I had little understanding of the community. I might have known something about American history, but I knew little of the local history of the district. I might have understood and could speak to state and national issues, but I did not understand how important it was to build relationships within the community. Nor did I have any local relationships. Not one. I had zeal but not much else to launch a political career.

You may desire to make a difference as well. In fact, I believe that within the DNA of followers of Jesus is the desire to make a difference and glorify God. We're made to walk with God and love and honor Him with our lives. He made us to love and serve our neighbors. One way of doing this is by serving in public office. By no means is it the only way to make a difference. It is for some. But before I could be ready to run for office, I had a lot of maturing to do.

Reflection: If you're considering a run for office, ask yourself: Are you mature enough? Is it the right time in your life? How would a run for office affect your family? Have you met with current elected leaders to seek their counsel? Have you prayed about it? Have you sought guidance from your pastor and mature believers from your church?

Let the wise hear and increase in learning, and the one who understands obtain guidance.
Proverbs 1:5

existed, but I've been in this field for 28 years and have thoroughly enjoyed it. I see it as a calling and will remain here as long as He keeps me in this field.

Reflection: Are you open to God's plan in your life? Are you willing to serve Him where He calls you? Do you trust Him to open doors to where He can best use you and your talents for the furthering of His kingdom?

∾

*Many are the plans in the mind of a man, but it is
the purpose of the Lord that will stand.*
Proverbs 19:21

3

GOD ORCHESTRATES EVENTS

Fifteen years after my initial meeting with Minority Leader Wilkins in Virginia, I was elected to the Trigg County (Kentucky) Fiscal Court as a magistrate. There was an open seat for a magistrate in my district, and after talking with a few key people, including the incumbent who was retiring, I decided to run. After encouraging good people to run for office over the years, I was simply taking my own advice. Little did I know that election to local office would propel me into a much more consequential political role in Kentucky.

After serving in office for a short time, I was catching up with a friend who started a Political Action Committee (PAC) called Family First Kentucky. She talked about her successes in her first year. I shared that I enjoyed serving in county government but sensed there was more I could offer to make a difference for the Commonwealth. After a distinct pause in the conversation, she said, "Richard, my family needs more of my attention, and I can't continue leading Family First. I've been praying for someone to take over, and you'd be the perfect person to lead it!" That came out of the blue and caught me by surprise.

Even though it had not crossed my mind to leave my position as a field representative with The Family Foundation of Kentucky, where I had worked for 14 years, I realized I had reached the ceiling in my role. I had a stable job—one that I did well. I also had a reliable income that my family depended upon. Wouldn't it be risky to start something new?

My friend convinced me to talk to a few people who helped her launch Family First. After several conversations and meetings with key people—political advisors, potential funders, and an election law attorney—I was ready to start the Commonwealth Policy Center (CPC). The transition was both complicated and interesting. Disentangling from my 14-year tenure as a field rep for what may be perceived as a competing organization would be tricky. Little did I know how interesting it was about to become.

In late 2011, one of the largest supporters of the organization I was working for at the time asked me to join him for an important meeting with some other state leaders to strategize how to defeat gambling expansion in the next legislative session. The meeting would be held at his business in Lexington, the same building that hosted my current employer. My boss would be at the meeting and determine which staff would attend such meetings. My presence at the meeting at the behest of someone else might cause consternation.

Here's where it gets interesting. During our meeting, the host suggested that the way to move the political needle in our direction and stop gambling expansion was through recruiting conservative, anti-gambling candidates. "We have two people in this room who'd do a good job recruiting. One is Reggie. The other is Richard. Richard, would you be willing to take a leave of absence and recruit candidates?" Of course, I answered yes. Then he looked to his right, where my boss was sitting, and asked if he would be willing to allow me to take a leave of absence. He agreed. How could he say no? His group's headquarters were donated by the host, one of the group's largest and most faithful donors.

The meeting was pivotal, and the results were very much unexpected. In a matter of minutes, potential obstacles with my current boss were smoothed over, and I was on a new path toward influencing statewide politics. This meeting and the intermediate job of candidate recruitment that I didn't go looking for but accepted nonetheless were the springboard that eventually helped launch CPC, the first ever full-time, socially conservative 501c4 in the Commonwealth of Kentucky. It provided a seamless transition for me, and I didn't have a clue the meeting would transpire that way.

Ultimately, God had His hand on that meeting, just as He stirred my soul a year earlier to explore the possibility of launching a new organization and taking on a bigger challenge. I don't believe in coincidences. I believe God was in that meeting just as much as He was in the phone conversation with my friend who led Family First and believed that I'd be a great fit. It was clear that God orchestrated all of these events. I was seeing the truth of Proverbs 16:9 playing out in real time: "The heart of man plans his way, but the Lord establishes his steps."

Reflection: Do you believe God orchestrates events? Have you considered how God is orchestrating events in your life? To push a metaphor, have you considered that you're an instrument in God's grand symphony? Have you asked Him to work in you and through you?

The plans of the heart belong to man, but the
answer of the tongue is from the Lord. . . .
Commit your work to the Lord, and
your plans will be established.
Proverbs 16:1, 3

4

GOD CALLS

"I don't know how you're able to deal with these tough issues," my friend said as he looked at me from behind his desk. He ran a successful Ford dealership in western Kentucky and was weary of recent disturbing news stories indicating a culture in trouble. I had led CPC for ten years, and my response to him was that I believed that God called me to this work. In fact, I couldn't do this work unless I was called to it.

I shared with my friend that the original vision I had for CPC was to do public policy through a biblical worldview— to look at the issues of the day through a biblical grid with the reality that God is at work and calls His people to be salt and light (Matthew 5:13–16) and disciple the nations (Matthew 28:18–20). Specifically, CPC's goal was to shore up the pillars of society: the sanctity of human life, marriage between one man and one woman, religious freedom, and fiscal integrity. These issues are often considered of little importance in light of prevailing secular values. These are contentious issues that are challenging to engage in the public arena. Issues like homosexual marriage, transgender identity, and abortion are like dynamite. There is little room for error; mishandling conversations around these issues can lead to disastrous consequences.

Have you ever considered what makes a society strong? Have you ever considered your core beliefs? What ideas and values are foundational to your life? It's important to reflect on this since our values and core beliefs shape who we are as people, how we live our lives, and how we act toward others.

How would you describe yourself? I'm a follower of Jesus. I'm also a work in progress. These are two ways to describe me. I also believe that God is at work and speaks to us through His Word, the Bible. I believe that the Bible isn't just any book; it is God's revelation of Himself (Hebrews 1) and His Son Jesus, the wellspring of truth and life (John 7:37–38). God's Word "is living and active, sharper than any two-edged sword, piercing to the division of soul and of spirit, of joints and of marrow, and discerning the thoughts and intentions of the heart" (Hebrews 4:12). The Bible speaks to all areas of life. Jesus calls His followers to follow Him wholeheartedly. These are my core beliefs. How about you?

Are you following God's call on your life?

According to Frederick Buechner, "The place God calls you to is the place where your deep gladness and the world's deep hunger meet."[1] Perhaps you are fulfilling your calling right now. Or perhaps God may be calling you to something else. You might be doing good things in your life, but is it where you find your deepest gladness? Are your skills and talents being used to fill the world's deepest hunger?

"When your hands are full, they are not open to the next thing God has for you." I can't remember exactly when I first heard those words, but they stuck with me. When I was elected in 2010 to serve a four-year term as 5th District Magistrate in Trigg County, I realized I had to let go of something. My time was even more limited now that I held a public office.

After much thought and prayer, I believed the best thing was to close my taxidermy shop, a labor of love that helped provide for my family. I ran it for 12 years. For a few of those years, my son was at my side, but I sensed God was calling me to use my time in a way that would have a greater impact for His kingdom. It was difficult to close the shop, a place where creativity and entrepreneurship met. I had a loyal group of customers, and I enjoyed turning their trophies into wildlife artistry and memories of a lifetime. But it was time to close that chapter of my life and open a new one. After all, God was writing my story, and it was clear that He was writing a new chapter.

Years after closing the shop, I'd occasionally get calls from customers asking me to mount one of their trophies. Obviously, I'd come a long way since I did work for my teenage friends, but it was clear that God was calling me to something else. This meant I'd have to let go of a perfectly good thing that I thoroughly enjoyed doing. It was a step of faith, and I'd soon find out the next thing He had in store for me.

Reflection: You may be doing good things with your life, but have you asked if they are the best things? Are you doing what God made you to do? You may make good money. You may hold a prestigious position. You may have all you've asked for in life, but here's the question: Are you devoting your life to what God called you to do? The answer may very well be yes. Yet consider whether it is God's calling on your life.

~

*To every thing there is a season, and a time to
every purpose under the heaven.*
Ecclesiastes 3:1

PART II

A CHRISTIAN APPROACH TO THE PUBLIC SQUARE

In conversation, lead with grace and land on the truth.

5

BEGIN IN PRAYER

"How are we going to find a principled conservative candidate to run for that seat?" I asked no one in particular in the summer of 2015. The state House seat that covered most of Owensboro, the fourth largest city in the Commonwealth, was held by a man who didn't represent the district's values. No longer pro-life, he had become a rubber stamp for any issue pushed by the unscrupulous Speaker of the House. "Why don't we gather a group of pastors and business leaders and pray?" That's just what we did. We filled the private dining room at Colby's Fine Food & Spirits, and I made a case as to why Owensboro needed better leadership. I opened the floor for Q&A and closed in prayer.

The meeting could have been just another meeting if we hadn't agreed to reconvene soon. To my surprise, three new people showed up at the next meeting and introduced themselves as candidates! Apparently, word traveled fast. Matt Castlen announced that he would challenge Democratic incumbent Tommy Thompson. It would be a longshot to unseat Thompson, a popular incumbent who previously served in a powerful leadership post. It wasn't the race we were focusing on, but nobody was complaining. Another candidate (who would eventually bow out of the race) also introduced himself to this group he learned had been praying for a candidate. Then DJ Johnson, who lived in the district where we needed a candidate, introduced himself. He was the one we were praying for.

Johnson was a former US Army veteran who operated a car wash—not exactly the kind of work that screams "political all-star approaching." But he had other, more important qualities. He was a diligent worker and active in his church. He had humility and was teachable. He had core convictions that he could defend, shared the values of the Christian community, and cared about his community in general. He was our guy—the guy we believed God raised up. After much hard work, DJ unseated the incumbent by 264 votes. Oh—Matt Castlen also won his race by nearly a 2 to 1 margin.

Both were part of a freshman class that made history by bringing a Republican majority to the state House for the first time in nearly 100 years. There is power in prayer. Elisabeth Elliot said, "Prayer lays hold of God's plan and becomes the link between his will and its accomplishment on earth. . . . Amazing things happen, and we are given the privilege of being the channels of the Holy Spirit's prayer."[1] God answers the prayers of His people when those prayers are ordered rightly. Quite frankly, God's people don't ask for enough.

Reflection: When making important decisions in your life, do you begin in prayer? Do you truly seek God's wisdom when making important decisions? Do you believe that God answers prayer? How do you respond when the answer to your prayer is not what you wanted?

You do not have, because you do not ask.
You ask and do not receive, because you ask
wrongly, to spend it on your passions.
James 4:2b–3

6

LEAD WITH GRACE, LAND ON TRUTH

There are three beliefs that allow me to engage the most difficult issues and opponents with grace. First, each of us is made in God's image (Genesis 1:26–28). Therefore, each of us is endowed with dignity and has infinite value in God's eyes. This includes my adversaries.

The second is that we are all sinners (Romans 3:23). I'm a sinner, just as my opponents are. As Francis Schaeffer once said, "There are two kinds of people in the world. Those who are at war with God and those who used to be at war with Him." This means that I was once at war with God.

The third reality is the gracious heart of God. It grips me that even while I was still steeped in rebellion against Him, He gave His life up for me. Romans 5:8 says, "While we were yet sinners, Christ died for us." I can identify with an opponent of the gospel because I was once a fellow adversary of God.

Jesus came to take away the sins of the world—my sin and your sin—when you put your faith in Him. Yet just because I've been saved from the consequences of my sin doesn't mean that I can be arrogant or feel superior to anyone else. Being set free from my sin wasn't something I did on my own. I didn't achieve forgiveness, nor did I deserve His grace. It's all about what Christ did on the cross for me. His life for mine. His righteousness for my unrighteousness. His suffering for my relief from suffering.

When these truths sink deep into the marrow of my soul, I realize that I must be compassionate and gracious to those still at war with their Creator. This is the key application followers of Jesus must embrace: the extent of God's grace grasped in one's life must be extended to others. This is the rubber meets the road of the second great commandment to love our neighbors as ourselves (Mark 12:31). This must be lived out in our daily lives.

Reflection: Are you gracious toward those still mired in their sin? Are you willing to step out of your comfort zone to share God's love with those adamantly opposed to the gospel?

The LGBTQ+ Identified Christian

I was giving a talk on the biblical view of marriage and the implications of redefining it. A conservative church had asked me to speak on this very important topic since the Supreme Court was considering a significant case that had the potential to change the nation's marriage laws.

In the middle of my message, several people got up and walked out. I thought, "Oh great." After the service, I was at the exit greeting people when a young woman approached me and asked, "Why are you hating on my people?" She wanted to debate me right there. I responded that this wasn't the time to debate since there were others waiting, but here's my card; give me a call, and we'll get together over coffee sometime.

I didn't expect her to call, but she contacted me later that afternoon, and we set up a time to talk the next day. When I arrived, there were three people there instead of just one. All glared at me. The tension was thick, and after making introductions, I said, "Look, this can be a really good meeting, or it can be a really bad meeting. If we argue and try to prove each other wrong, it will end up being a bad meeting. But if we listen to one another and try to understand each other's stories, it can be a good meeting. How about we try to have a good meeting?"

Across from me was a self-identified lesbian with a pink Bible. The other two looked at me suspiciously. At that point, I decided to put aside all the Bible verses that spoke of marriage and homosexual behavior, and I just listened to her story. She told me about growing up in church, accepting Christ at a young age, but then falling into sin in her high school years. The church eventually kicked her out. By the time of our meeting, she was in a long-term lesbian relationship.

The way she described her significant other as supportive and caring stood out. She stated, "My partner is my everything, and I couldn't go on without her." When it was my turn to speak, I shared some of my story. I made clear that I was a sinner like she was. "But my sin is not your sin, and your sin is not my sin," I said. "But we are both sinners. I cannot relate to your story. But if you believe that book next to you, it says that if you are in Christ, He is your everything. In fact, He is your new identity." The words hung in the air. I don't know what she did after that, but all I could offer was compassion and grace. I believe listening to her and genuinely caring about her and her story opened the door for the gospel. It was the truth she needed to hear.

Reflection: Are you willing to sit down with someone who identifies as LGBTQ+ and listen to their story? Are you willing to offer them both compassion and the truth? Have you asked God to use you specifically to reach the hurting and broken in the LGBTQ+ community? Is there something in your life that is your everything—but isn't Jesus?

Therefore, if anyone is in Christ, he is a new creation. The old has passed away; behold, the new has come.
2 Corinthians 5:17

Respect and Civility Are Magnetic

I made the case on Kentucky Tonight that "Fairness" laws aren't fair when they can be used against nonprofit groups like Sunrise Children's Services, who had a right to craft employment policies consistent with their religious convictions. Sunrise was under attack from Kentucky LGBTQ+ activists who were trying to cancel them—and their state contract—simply because they required employees to abide by a code of Christian sexual ethics. When a Sunrise employee publicly identified as a lesbian, it resulted in her firing.

The oldest foster care and child placement agency in the Commonwealth faced harsh criticism from the mainstream news media. Under Governor Steve Beshear's administration, Sunrise's prospect of losing its state contract loomed. On Kentucky Educational Television (KET), an hour-long live weekly program, the most visible cheerleader for gay rights in the Commonwealth kept interrupting me. He was rude and condescending. As tough as it was, by God's grace, I remained calm and tried to be as respectful as possible while still making the points that needed to be made. It was painful, but the bright studio lights that shone on the participants also reflected my opponent's ugly attitude toward religious freedom and conscience rights.

Later that week, I received an unexpected phone call from a Louisville attorney who openly identified as homosexual. He was upset at how I was treated with disdain by someone who was supposed to represent LGBTQ+ rights. As he later shared, "It was the contempt I saw in ███████████ on KET Tonight that made me reach out . . . and try to do something that was honestly based on 'fairness.'"

He and I later met over coffee, and he shared his story with me. I shared a bit of my story, including my faith convictions. It was a respectful conversation and encouraging to know that civility between people with very different views on a controversial issue is still possible.

The meeting eventually opened the door to an invitation to speak to the Kentucky Bar Association's Diversity and Inclusion Summit, an event conservative groups aren't usually part of. Yet the door was open, reminding me that respect and civility can make someone lean in a little to better hear what you're saying.

. . .

Reflection: Are you willing to respectfully engage people with opposing views? Does your tone and the way you interact with opponents honor your Savior? Are you committed to raising the bar of civility?

Pray also for us, that God may open to us a door for the word,
to declare the mystery of Christ, on account
of which I am in prison—that I may make it
clear, which is how I ought to speak.
Walk in wisdom toward outsiders, making the best use
of the time. Let your speech always be gracious,
seasoned with salt, so that you may know
how you ought to answer each person.
Colossians 4:3–6

7

THE IMPORTANCE OF VISION

I spoke at a fundraising event in early 2022 for Boyle County Judge-Executive Howard Hunt, a friend of mine. After telling the audience why they should re-elect Judge Hunt and contribute to his campaign, I shared a few observations about the challenge to our nation. I told the group that the political left has cast a vision for the nation's future, including free healthcare for all, a Green New Deal, student loan forgiveness, and basic minimum income. Their idea of human rights is predicated on a radical self-autonomy that manifests itself socially in sexual libertinism. In this view, there is no room for God. The left has cast a vision and, in fact, implemented much of it. "What is the conservative vision?" I asked the upper middle class conservative audience. "Is there even a conservative vision?" It caught a few people off guard and shocked a few, but it made them think.

Republicans, who largely represent socially conservative principles regarding human nature in American politics, are often considered the "party of no." I once heard Grover

Norquist talk about the factions that bind together the conservative movement: Second Amendment advocates, small business owners, and the No More Taxes crowd. He called the collective group the "Leave Us Alone Coalition."[1] While each issue is important to conservatives, a cantankerous tone and defensive posture are not a vision. Until the conservative movement moves from its defensive foxholes to a proactive posture that casts a vision of human flourishing and what it means to be a good society, it will continue to lose ground.

Christians understand the idea of vision. "Where there is no vision, the people perish" (Proverbs 29:18a KJV). Scripture says that if you don't have a vision for your future, it doesn't matter which road you'll take to get there (Matthew 7:13–14). If you don't have a vision for a politically healthy nation, it doesn't matter which party you support or who is in power. The Bible has a vision for the good life and the good society. The good life is marked by love, joy, peace, patience, kindness, goodness, faithfulness, and self-control. The good society is marked by citizens free to pursue the good, the true, and the beautiful. It is tempered by justice and mercy.

Scripture tells us who man is, why he was created, and how he ought to live if he is to flourish. The Bible gives a path of spiritual health and a vision for true life. It tells us about the future reality found in Revelation 21:1–4:

> Then I saw a new heaven and a new earth, for the first heaven and the first earth had passed away, and the sea was no more. And I saw the holy city, new Jerusalem, coming down out of heaven from God, prepared as a bride adorned for her husband. And I heard a loud voice from the throne saying, "Behold, the dwelling place of God is with man. He

will dwell with them, and they will be his people, and God himself will be with them as their God. He will wipe away every tear from their eyes, and death shall be no more, neither shall there be mourning, nor crying, nor pain anymore, for the former things have passed away."

Reflection: Do you have a biblical vision for life? What is your vision of politics? Is your vision influenced by knowing how God has worked through history and that He is still at work today? Does your political vision bend toward a Revelation 21 reality of a new heaven and a new earth?

∼

Where there is no vision, the people perish.
Proverbs 29:18a KJV

8

LOVING YOUR ENEMIES
IS MANDATORY

The most contentious issue CPC engages in is "Fairness" ordinances. These ordinances make LGBTQ+ identity a protected class in the areas of housing, employment, and public accommodations. Interestingly, in most cases where they're introduced, there are exactly zero documented cases of discrimination based on someone's sexual orientation. Of course, this makes the laws unnecessary and extremely divisive. When such proposals are introduced to local governments, fear and contention are around the corner. They bring about conflict and sometimes reveal bad theology and uncharitable behavior from the Christian community.

Such was the case when I was invited to speak to a concerned group of citizens in Augusta in early 2021. As soon as I got out of my car, I knew it would be a long evening in this tight-knit northern Kentucky community nestled along the banks of the Ohio River. I heard the chanting across the street. Lining the sidewalk across the street from the church holding the meeting were dozens of animated LGBTQ+ activists holding placards.

The Kentucky Fairness Campaign orchestrated the response, as they usually do. As I made my way to the church, Fairness Campaign leader Chris Hartman approached and greeted me with his trademark hug. "Good to see you, Richard," Hartman said. Chris and I had debated in public forums over the years. I talked to him for a minute and invited him into the church to hear what I had to say. After all, what better place for an opponent of the gospel to be but in the church?

A Cincinnati TV station camera was recording the drama as I walked to the front of the church where a group of men were standing, presumably on guard. I asked if this was the right door for the meeting. "And who are you?" one asked. I told them I was invited to speak. He responded, "Which side are you on?" Another clue that this was going to be a long night.

While most of us would rather avoid such conflict, Christians are called to bring God's truth to the world (Matthew 28:18–20) and expose evil (Ephesians 5:11). Believers are called to shape culture by living out the principles of the faith. This means standing for truth in the public arena. But just as important as standing for truth is standing for truth in the right way, a God-honoring way. Humiliation, name-calling, and bigotry should have no place in a Christian's life. Period. Full stop.

When I settled into the front pew, I wasn't prepared for the outright anger and hostility aimed at the LGBTQ+ activists chanting across the street. There was no compassion toward them, nor a call to pray for them. When I began to speak, I suggested that those across the street howling at us needed God's love and compassion as much as I did.

I explained to the group that when we engage in public issues, our maxim is to lead with grace and land on truth. Followers of Jesus should begin in a place of great humility because sinners bring nothing to God and do nothing to merit His saving power in their lives. It's all grace. It's all Him. As we grasp this, it should result in tremendous humility when we engage others.

"I'm still learning how to love my enemies in the context of the public arena," I told the group. I could still hear the chants from across the street. Jesus tells us to love our enemies: "But I say to you who hear, Love your enemies, do good to those who hate you, bless those who curse you, pray for those who abuse you" (Luke 6:27–28). However difficult it may be, Jesus demands this of His followers.

The Q&A time was interesting. One of the deacons bristled at my appeal to be kind and gracious to the opposition. He essentially said homosexuals don't deserve grace until they "clean themselves up so God could accept them." An older woman miffed that I didn't call fire down from heaven insinuated that I might actually be a homosexual. "We don't need you to come here and talk about the Bible," said the pastor of the church hosting the meeting. "We want to know what the Constitution says." The pastor walked out shortly after. In my humiliation, I cut short the Q&A. I was grieved and embarrassed for that church.

I witnessed firsthand Francis Schaeffer's words: "There is nothing more ugly than an orthodoxy without understanding or without compassion."[1] They embraced a carpet-bombing approach at the expense of biblical passages like 2 Timothy 2:24–26: "And the Lord's servant must not be quarrelsome but kind to everyone, able to teach, patiently enduring evil, correcting his opponents with gentleness. God may perhaps grant them repentance leading to a knowledge of the truth, and they may come to their senses and escape from the snare of the devil, after being captured by him to do his will."

There is an enemy, but we forget who he is and that he captures people to do his will. Targeting the protestors outside the church as the ultimate enemy is akin to targeting a POW. We don't shoot prisoners of war. We try to free them, as Paul said, "from the snare of the devil." The church can do better. After all, Jesus suffered to free us. We are free, therefore, to help free others.

Reflection: Have you ever found yourself speaking to a difficult group where you're standing against a strong headwind of ugliness? How have you responded? Have you considered that God uses His people in challenging environments? Are you willing to be used by Him?

You have heard that it was said,
"You shall love your neighbor and hate your enemy."
But I say to you, Love your enemies and pray for those who
persecute you, so that you may be sons
of your Father who is in heaven.
Matthew 5:43–45a

9
———————

CONSEQUENCES OF SUBMITTING
TO POLITICAL LEADERS

I n the spring of 2020, we were in the early stages of the coronavirus pandemic. Governor Andy Beshear issued an executive order that ordered most businesses to close. I sent an open letter to Kentucky churches with suggestions, including encouraging them to pray for the governor. Governor Beshear acknowledged my open letter while at the same time acknowledging that we likely disagreed on most issues. Another political adversary, Paducah Mayor Brandi Harless, obtained a copy of the letter and read it publicly. In part, this is what I said:

> Are you praying for the health of your community and for the disease to slow? Then do something to help effectuate that prayer. Are you asking God to give our leaders wisdom? Then please know the same Bible that tells us to pray for our leaders in 1 Timothy 2:1 tells us also to submit to those same leaders (Romans 13:1 and 1 Peter 2:13–17).

> Jesus reminds us that the two great commandments are to love God and love our neighbor (Matthew 22:36–40).

Submitting to our government honors God. Following the stay-at-home order and practicing social distancing to help slow the spread is loving our neighbor.

So, should you hold in-person church services this Easter Sunday? Simply ask yourself this: Do you want to be remembered as being the conduit that spread a deadly disease throughout a region? Or do you want to be remembered as being a force for good that aided your community in a time of great need?

Early on, we knew very little about the transmissibility and impact COVID-19 would have on certain populations. Governments and health professionals are charged to lead in a time of public health crisis. Praying for wisdom and deferring to their leadership is a biblical response. I led in a way that I thought best honored God. However, not all agreed. Shortly after the open letter circulated, I was disinvited to participate in a Christian radio show even though I'd previously been a frequent guest. However, I was invited to join one of Kentucky's most listened-to morning programs. Isn't that interesting?

To lead is often controversial on some level. This is because human beings reflexively resist authority. However, Christians should earnestly submit to government authorities. The only exception is when authorities usurp the things that are God's (Acts 5:29). When the biblical response doesn't fit a political narrative and political commitment, pursue the biblical response but be prepared to pay a price. You may be harshly criticized and even slandered. It may cost some friendships and political alliances, but it's a price worth paying if done in good faith and in honor to God.

Reflection: Does Scripture inform your response to government more than your political commitments? Have you ever stood against the currents of your own political tribe to stand on biblical truth? What are biblical lines you will refuse to cross if your political tribe demands it? Are you willing to pay a price?

∼

Let your reasonableness be known to everyone.
The Lord is at hand.
Philippians 4:5

10

THE SPIRITUAL WAR BEHIND POLITICAL BATTLES

Every four years in this nation, there's a contest for the presidency. Every two years, there's a fight for control of Congress. These are political battles. The candidates will campaign on the issues. They will propose solutions to issues like homelessness, drug addiction, and crime. Yet any solution, however well intended, will fall far short of fixing the problem when it neglects the limits of what government can do and simultaneously rejects the spiritual realities behind each of these issues.

Consider the crisis of human pain and brokenness in our nation. Drug addiction and overdose deaths are both at epidemic levels. Homelessness is a crisis in our major cities. Suicide is the second leading cause of death among teenagers. Loneliness has been declared a health crisis. What is going on? We are the wealthiest and freest nation in history, yet so much despair surrounds us. Our day is eerily similar to Savinus's observations of Rome in the fifth century: "The Roman empire is luxurious but it is filled with misery. It is dying, but it laughs."

Hundreds of millions of dollars are being spent on the drug addiction crisis. In fact, Kentucky recently received over $400 million to address opioid addiction.[1] But, as I shared with the administrator of this government program, we will be falling far short if we neglect Christian ministries that deal with the heart and soul issues leading to addiction in the first place. Political solutions based primarily on money are limited because they are centered on material needs. While sometimes helpful, they will never solve a crisis that is, at its core, spiritual. Left in a state of sin and alienation from God, we are captive to our flesh and its rigorous demands at the expense of our souls.

The biblical worldview teaches us that a spiritual battle rages behind the scenes every day. Paul told the church in Ephesus, "We do not wrestle against flesh and blood, but against the rulers, against the authorities, against the cosmic powers over this present darkness, against the spiritual forces of evil in the heavenly places" (Ephesians 6:12). Paul casts a vision for believers to fit themselves with spiritual armaments: the belt of truth, the breastplate of righteousness, as shoes—readiness given by the gospel of peace, the shield of faith, the helmet of salvation, and God's Word, which is the sword of the Spirit (Ephesians 6:13–18). Such armaments seemed foolish in the face of fierce Roman legions, who could crush people in an instant. Yet the courage and faith of the early church overcame the spiritual hollowness of a Roman civilization whose tenets were at war with the Living God.

Many Christians were killed because they refused to burn incense to Caesar. They acknowledged a greater reality outside of his temporal rule. As a result, some were martyred, and their deaths shed light on a greater reality of the spiritual war over who deserves ultimate allegiance. Caesar is still in the grave. Christ has risen. Who do you follow?

The way you answer that question will determine how you will live. Followers of Jesus are on a path to live radically different lives, and they engage the world in a radically different way. Their lives are imbued with love, joy, peace, patience, kindness, goodness, faithfulness, gentleness, and self-control (Galatians 5:22–23). Believers are marked by "compassionate hearts, kindness, humility, meekness, and patience, bearing with one another and . . . forgiving each other . . . . And above all these [believers] put on love, which binds everything together in perfect harmony. And let the peace of Christ rule in your hearts, to which indeed you were called in one body" (Colossians 3:12–15). It becomes clear that as a Christian's character grows, it tempers how they engage others. A Christian's ultimate hope is not merely in a government solution but in the restoration of their soul by the Living God. And their marching orders are to love God and love their neighbors as themselves.

Instead of seeing political power as the only means to restore society to health, there are many opportunities to minister to the hurting and broken all around, including those devastated by the sexual revolution, women who have been abused through exploitation, and orphaned and trafficked children who need families. There are as many opportunities for Christians today as there were for the early church.

There is clearly a war going on, but the weapons Christians fight with aren't the same kind the world uses. They're otherworldly weapons, spiritual in nature, and have the power to really change lives. And when lives are miraculously changed, so is the political calculus. For Christians filled with the Spirit, the most important weapon we can wield is love.

Reflection: When you engage in current issues, do you acknowledge spiritual realities? Have you asked God to clothe you with spiritual armor and to help you engage battles according to His rules of warfare? Or has your tendency been to wage war as the world does? Have you considered how you can bring biblical truths to bear on the pressing issues of today?

For though we live in the world, we do not wage war as the world does. The weapons we fight with are not the weapons of the world. On the contrary, they have divine power to demolish strongholds. We demolish arguments and every pretension that sets itself up against the knowledge of God, and we take captive every thought to make it obedient to Christ.
2 Corinthians 10:3–5

PART III

SHAPED BY TRIALS

11

FAILURE DOESN'T DEFINE YOU

Ulysses S. Grant graduated near the bottom of his class at West Point and eventually went bankrupt in business. Abraham Lincoln lost three elections, and when he eventually became president, he was lampooned by the news media as an ape. Albert Einstein's grade-school teacher told his mother that he was incapable of learning and wouldn't amount to much. Humanity would have lost if any one of them had given in to their critics or stayed stuck in their failures, real or perceived.

A Christian radio station manager in Bowling Green and I would do occasional programs on the Kentucky General Assembly. At one point, I asked him if he ever thought about running for the legislature. It was one of a handful of conversations I had with him about politics and running for office. He told me about his past as a marine who was Semper Fi to all the things not considered exemplary in life. Part of his story, however, was the powerful transformation in his life when he began following Jesus. He ended up pastoring a church, managing a Christian radio station, and eventually decided not to let his past keep him out of politics. He ended up running for the state Senate and unseated an incumbent in a long-shot race. Sen. Mike Wilson told his story at a CPC event, sharing how his past was filled with things he wasn't proud of and how he "went from the gutter-most to the uttermost."

Do you think your past prevents you from moving ahead to do great acts of service? The enemy would like to define you and convince you that you are tainted—a hypocrite and totally unusable to God. The truth is, you are of inestimable value and worth in God's eyes. When you come to Jesus Christ, you are no longer defined by sin, shame, and failure. Jesus gives you a new beginning and a new reference point on how to live life. Once you've come to faith in Christ, your past is history, and it does not define your personhood. This is because you have a new identity in Christ. The person you were is dead. When you put on a new life in Christ, He gives you a new purpose. Remember that when you've come to faith in Jesus, He's the one writing your story, not the enemy.

Even if you run for office or some other position of influence, don't be afraid to use your story and the willingness to be vulnerable, which has its own power. This is Dan Allender's thesis in his book *Leading with a Limp*.[1] By God's grace, allow Him to work through the soul-shaping trials in your life otherwise called failures. You can achieve victory over what you believe is a ruined life filled with disappointment. I'm reminded of Angela Minter, once radically pro-abortion, who had two abortions of her own. She now leads a powerful pro-life ministry in Louisville called Sisters for Life. Daniel Mingo, who struggled with homosexual sin for years, was supernaturally freed from his sin and has a ministry in Louisville to those struggling with sexual sin today. We've all failed and fallen short of God's glory, but our story doesn't need to end there.

Oh, that guy who was reluctant to run for office and eventually got elected to the state Senate won a leadership post and was key in helping restore a sanctity of life ethic in the Commonwealth. So, if your past is holding you back from putting yourself out there to serve and make a difference, think again, "for it is God who works in you, both to will and to work for His good pleasure" (Philippians 2:13).

Reflection: Do your past failures define you? Or are you defined by God, who is shaping your life? Are you willing to share your story with others and help build them up? Are you willing to give your failures to God and allow Him to work through them?

Not only that, but we rejoice in our sufferings, knowing that suffering produces endurance, and endurance produces character, and character produces hope, and hope does not put us to shame, because God's love has been poured into our hearts through the Holy Spirit who has been given to us.
Romans 5:3–5

12

GROWTH WITHIN THE CRUCIBLE
OF POLITICAL ATTACKS

I was traveling on the Western Kentucky Parkway when I took a call from someone I met a year or two earlier at a fundraising luncheon. I don't usually take random calls, but I recognized the name and answered. "Richard, I don't know if you remember me, but we met some time ago. I need to tell you that I'm really upset with you. I was told that you spoke to a group and said that my daughter is having an affair with ███████." The guy he named happened to be an influential politician and leading candidate in a race for the most powerful political office in Kentucky.

I was taken aback, and a flurry of emotions coursed through my veins as I listened. Disbelief, anger, and outrage converged in a single moment. What do you do with a call like that? This wasn't some kind of political malcontent. He was an influential and credible person who was politically connected. He had a close family member working for a high-level political leader, and I tried to quickly figure out what to make of the call.

I could have become defensive and angry. However, responding in anger never helps. Fortunately, calmness and clear thinking prevailed and allowed me to respond, "Well, that's not how I do things. If you talk to people who know me, you'll find out the same. Here's what I suggest you do: please talk to whoever you heard that from and ask them which group I spoke to and when I supposedly said those things. This will help me with some context. And let me know what you find." He called me back a couple of weeks later with an apology, admitting the rumor had no basis.

Charles Spurgeon once said, "The best way to deal with slander is to pray about it: God will either remove it, or remove the sting from it. Our own attempts at clearing ourselves are usually failures; we are like the boy who wished to remove the blot from his copy, and by his bungling made it ten times worse."[1]

Reflection: Have you ever been slandered before? How have you responded? Have you sought God's guidance as to the best response? The truth will eventually be known, even if not in this lifetime. Do you trust God to exonerate you?

> *Having a good conscience, so that, when you*
> *are slandered, those who revile your good*
> *behavior in Christ may be put to shame.*
> *1 Peter 3:16*

Addressing False Accusations

Have you ever been wrongly accused of something? It's never pleasant. It's even more troubling when state legislators misrepresent you after you've given testimony to a legislative committee. Such was the case when my friend and pastor

Hershael York and I testified in the summer of 2020 in front of the Veterans, Military Affairs, and Public Protection Committee about Gov. Andy Beshear's disregard for religious liberty during his COVID shutdown.

Gov. Beshear ordered state police to record the license plate numbers of church attendees who met in person for Easter services contrary to his orders. I shared a story relayed by a pastor friend in Hopkinsville about a state police cruiser stationed in the median where cars turn to enter the parking lot—an intimidating move for churchgoers who've never seen a police car there before. Churches were declared "nonessential" entities weeks earlier. (The state legislature eventually passed a law in the 2022 General Assembly Session declaring that churches were indeed essential to the community).

Shortly after, two Democratic legislators on the committee wrote a memo to their colleagues charging that I gave false and misleading testimony. This is the death knell to anyone in the political world. Lose your credibility, and you lose your place of influence. I was incensed after reading the detailed memo. It was flat-out wrong and untrue.

My assistant and I immediately began working on a detailed response. I sent the three-page rebuttal to the committee chairman and asked him to circulate it to his colleagues on the entire committee. It took a while for me to cool down, but I did what was necessary. I left the rest in God's hands.

Reflection: How do you respond when falsely accused? Have you considered that when Jesus was falsely accused, sometimes He was silent? Are you at peace with God's vindication even if it's not clear to all in this lifetime?

Behold, I have created the smith who blows the fire of coals and produces a weapon for its purpose. I have also created the ravager to destroy; no weapon that is fashioned against you shall succeed, and you shall refute every tongue that rises against you in judgment. This is the heritage of the servants of the Lord and their vindication from me, declares the Lord.
Isaiah 54:16–17

Undeserved Curses

"I have zero respect for you and your organization after the column you wrote about my candidate." Thus began the email I received during the 2016 Republican presidential primary. "I want you to take me off your mailing list and don't ever contact me again." This abrupt email came from an obviously unhappy person. But it wasn't a random individual. He was an acquaintance and former financial supporter of CPC, and he was seriously upset over a column I wrote about the need for character in our political candidates, specifically presidential candidates vying for the 2016 nomination in the Republican primary.

We met at a fundraiser hosted by one of my board members. We had mutual friends. Our kids had played sports together and graduated in the same class. He appreciated our work to restore Christian values in the culture. He identified as a Christian, yet I was perplexed that my view on presidential primary candidates somehow justified such an uncharitable reaction.

A few years later, I walked into church a little late and scrambled to find a seat as the worship team was halfway through the first song. I spotted one down in front where I could slip in unnoticed. After the song ended, I looked to the person on my left; it was the same guy who excoriated me in the email a couple of years earlier. We eventually greeted one another and chatted for a few minutes after the service, but that was the last time I saw him at church.

Our opinions mean something. But for those who identify as followers of Jesus, opinions should take a back seat to treating others with respect and kindness. Treating others with dignity and respect is a rule in life, even if you oppose their beliefs. Your words matter. If you're tempted to use them wrongly in anger, hold your tongue. It is better to leave unsaid something that could really hurt someone than let angry words fly, only to be haunted by them in the future. When you make it a practice to treat charitably those with whom you disagree, you'll be able to live with yourself if one day you find yourself sitting next to them in church.

Reflection: Have you ever regretted using your words in an angry and condemning way? Do you hold your political opinions as sacred and more important than Christian principles of charity? How can you work on treating others with kindness and care in political conversations?

Like a sparrow in its flitting, like a swallow in its flying, a curse that is causeless does not alight.
Proverbs 26:2

Admitting Mistakes

Why is it so difficult to admit when you're wrong? We do not like to be wrong, and we do not like being told we're wrong. When criticized, we quickly get defensive. It's natural for us to protect ourselves. At best, we want to maintain our credibility and outward appearance. At worst, we are prideful and self-justify bad behavior.

The Pain-Capable Unborn Child Protection Act banned abortions after twenty weeks. Sen. Brandon Smith, sponsor of the bill, invited me to testify with him before a Senate Committee in 2017. My testimony was logical, supported by facts, and delivered in a compelling way. I was pleased with my testimony and believed that it brought light to the issue. Except for one thing. I made the error of not double-checking one of the points I made about legal challenges to similar laws in other states. I got my information from a national group that didn't update its information, and for that, I paid a price. My testimony was incomplete at best and misleading at worst.

The next day, a friend in the Senate brought the error to my attention. Andy Beshear, the attorney general at the time, shared a memo with Senators on the committee stating I had given inaccurate testimony. I actually think the language was more along the lines of "Richard Nelson with CPC gave false testimony." It stung to see those words written by the attorney general. Even now, I'm tempted to downplay it and blame the national organization I relied on for accurate information or even blame the pro-abortion attorney general's office.

It was painful to see my name and my organization implicated. But what about the 99 percent of the testimony that was compelling? That was good, but the 1 percent was what hurt. I'd learned a lesson to be more careful, double-check my sources, and own the mistake I made. Owning your mistakes is part of growing in character. The sooner you admit wrong and own it, the stronger you become in the long run.

Reflection: Is it hard for you to admit mistakes? What is stopping you from owning up to your mistakes and learning through them? What is God revealing to you through your mistakes?

~

Whoever conceals his transgressions will not prosper, but he who confesses and forsakes them will obtain mercy.
Proverbs 28:13

13

GOD WORKS THROUGH DEEP PAIN

The disclaimer statement about me was read from the pulpit of one of the largest churches in Paducah. Earlier in the week, the church had hosted my presentation on a proposed Sexual Orientation Gender Identity ordinance. During my speech, I said such ordinances remove a "spiritual covering from a community." Now, the church's disclaimer said that during my presentation, "Richard made a comment about a fundraiser put on by a nonprofit organization called Heart USA." The church supported the efforts of the nonprofit, which helped defray medical bills for those who needed help. What the statement didn't reveal to the congregation was that the nonprofit group planned to raise money through a womanless beauty contest. In other words, the group raised money by hosting a drag show.

Compounding the betrayal, the church's pastor knew me personally and appeared to side with the opposition. I eventually called him to clarify their reason for the statement. He told me one of the church families had a homosexual son, and they were offended by my presentation. The church's attorney, the one who wrote the disclaimer, was a personal friend. Just two months earlier, we were debating partners on a similar topic in another city.

In addition, an ally of the LGBTQ+ community snuck into the back of the church, secretly recorded my talk, and posted it on the internet, where it soon went viral. Shortly after, I was doxed. My private information was posted online. Vile attacks and threats were posted on CPC's social media pages. For two weeks, my staff monitored our Twitter and Facebook pages, scrubbed the filth, and blocked abusive users.

As if this wasn't painful enough, family members publicly condemned me, including my then father-in-law and wife. Earlier that year, my wife had posted statements on social media in favor of LGBTQ+ identity. The most hurtful betrayal came shortly after the Paducah church publicly distanced itself from me. I came home to a U-Haul truck parked in the driveway as my wife abruptly packed up for South Carolina.

Every one of us turned our back on the Redeemer of Mankind, making every one of us guilty of cosmic treason against the King of the Universe. Any betrayal we face in our personal lives pales in comparison to what Jesus faced. Thank God that His response wasn't "I'm going to crush them. I'm going to make them pay. I'll embarrass them." His response was to give His life up to redeem our lives (Romans 5:8).

These truths don't make personal betrayal sting any less. My hurt was accompanied by hot tears for a season. My primary and very real comfort was to know Jesus and know that He identified with my rejection and abandonment. Here's the amazing thing: not only did He understand and identify with what I endured, but He forgave me for my betrayal of Him.

This was deeply comforting. This is the foundation that afforded me the capacity to forgive those who deeply hurt me.

Reflection: How do you deal with hurt and betrayal? How do you deal with the deep pain that follows? How do you get past the temptation to become bitter? Have you considered that your betrayal of God is far greater than any betrayal you'll face here on earth?

Not that I have already obtained this or am already perfect, but I press on to make it my own, because Christ Jesus has made me his own. Brothers, I do not consider that I have made it my own. But one thing I do: forgetting what lies behind and straining forward to what lies ahead, I press on toward the goal for the prize of the upward call of God in Christ Jesus.
Philippians 3:12–14

14

PERSONAL BROKENNESS, PUBLIC SHAME

I t is very easy for those in ministry and public life who have led exemplary lives to build an image, not necessarily by design but often by default. This image takes shape over the course of many years in public ministry. Working for the right things and touching people's lives in heartfelt ways inevitably leads to the public's perception of a person. So, what happens when the public's perception of one's image shatters?

After several attempts at marriage counseling, a marriage retreat, and personal counseling from pastors, my marriage ended. I suffer no delusions that I'm without fault. After all, there are two people in a marriage, and both contribute to its success as much as its failure. I felt defeated. The defeat was magnified after she left for South Carolina to be closer to our oldest daughter and her family. The house—once filled with the hustle and bustle of activity, voices of my kids, tunes from the piano reverberating throughout the great room, and my youngest singing beautiful songs she'd improvised—was now quiet. It was still. And it was sad.

My daily routine began with morning coffee, time in Scripture, and meditation in my favorite place: the sunroom where I'd watch the sun rise every morning. The birds still came to the feeder just feet from the large window. The sun's rays shot through the tree line at the driveway's edge, bringing hope and warmth to a new day. Life went on as usual on the outside, even though my world was falling apart inside.

I contemplated leaving my work and ministry. One of the most humiliating things was to continue attending the church where we raised our kids. But where was I to go? I had many friends who loved me and visited me during that time. My pastor knew my story and counseled me. Where better to be? We were supposed to be a family, a family that should have a deeper affinity than biological family with blood ties.

It later dawned on me that to not return to my home church would have deprived them of an opportunity to minister to me. My biggest challenge was to replay events over and over in my mind and question what I could have done differently. I was beating myself up in a meeting with my pastor when he said, "Look, you may have done things differently, but it might not have changed a thing." I needed to hear that. British pastor and theologian Martyn Lloyd-Jones said, "If you are looking at your past and your sins and you are depressed, it means that you are *listening to the devil*."[1] I was listening to the devil way too much.

During one morning quiet time, a rushing wave of reality washed over me, almost as if a voice spoke to me: "The enemy meant this for evil. He meant to hurt you and take you out. But the enemy is not writing the rest of your story!" I asked God, "Do you really love me? Do you really care about me?" The answer came in the form of a resounding joy that filled my heart with a clear "Yes, I care about you deeply. Enough to give my life for you." The hope of the cross and the resurrection buoyed me, keeping me afloat when I felt like I was sinking. The One who rose from the grave revived me from grief and shame too heavy to bear. I've never felt closer to God, never felt His affection and care more than in the two years after the separation and divorce. And for this, I'm grateful.

Reflection: How do you face deep pain in your life? Have you trusted God to work through your pain? Have you seen good come from pain and evil?

In this you rejoice, though now for a little while, if
necessary, you have been grieved by various trials,
so that the tested genuineness of your faith—
more precious than gold that perishes though it
is tested by fire—may be found to result in
praise and glory and honor at the
revelation of Jesus Christ.
1 Peter 1:6–7

15

GOD WORKS THROUGH SUFFERING

Good can be worked through evil. Life comes from death. Purpose comes from participating in a bigger story outside of ourselves. These are biblical ideas. They are rooted in the story of Jesus, who overcame evil through humility and righteousness, defeated death through His death and resurrection, and fulfilled a purpose to renew and set aright a universe crippled by sin. Jesus suffered greatly and died an ignoble death without wealth, title, or power. By all worldly measures of what is considered leadership success, Jesus Christ was a miserable failure. Except He wasn't. He wasn't because His standard of success is far greater and outside our limited idea of success.

Jesus's sacrifice and servanthood define true leadership and success. Christ's infinite love first draws us and then binds us to Him, and it's through suffering that we grow closer to Him. When we allow God to work in us to redeem and use our suffering, life-changing and amazing things happen.

Consider my friend Gwendolyn. Her first child was diagnosed with trisomy 18 in the third trimester. When she heard the doctor say, "Your baby has a condition incompatible with life," she was devastated. The baby was born weeks later and lived less than an hour in the arms of her parents. They named her Hope.

Gwendolyn eventually started a pregnancy care center (PCC) in western Kentucky for women who had little to no support while carrying their unborn child. Door of Hope is a pro-life ministry, a response to a culture that says, "If you're not ready for a child, abortion is the solution." Baby Hope was the inspiration for a ministry that said otherwise. This ministry was born out of the reality of great pain and suffering and the loss of a precious child. Inspiration came from Hosea 2:15, "And there I will give her vineyards and make the Valley of Achor a door of hope."

These centers focus on caring for women, loving them, and walking alongside them in their time of need. There are approximately sixty PCCs across the Commonwealth and an estimated 2500 across the nation. These ministries have elevated the lives of the unborn and their mothers and have greatly contributed to winning over public opinion in favor of protecting unborn human life.

Gwendolyn could have turned inward and dwelt on her grief and pain, but instead, she allowed God to use it. As a result, hundreds—if not thousands of women—have been blessed through this ministry. She co-authored a book called *Threads of Hope, Pieces of Joy*, a pregnancy loss Bible study she shared with us when my wife lost our third child to a miscarriage.[1] We were young, nearly 700 miles from our closest family, and had few friends in the area. Gwendolyn came to the funeral to help us grieve.

The good that can come from suffering—if you let God work through it—is immeasurable. When you've tasted suffering, you will never judge harshly. I'll never look down on someone who's gone through a divorce. When you've suffered, you're more able to bear others' burdens, especially if you've suffered in the same way.

One of the most radical prayers is "Lord, make me more like you." I asked a friend how to draw closer to Jesus and become more like Him. He shared words of wisdom from Paul Washer, who said, "Get really, really, broken." But what if you want the Lord to use you in a great way? It's one of the most dangerous prayers because that heartfelt prayer just might be answered. Yet, it may be answered in a way that you least expect. After all, the Author of your life is writing your story, not you.

Reflection: You can allow suffering to shape you in one of two directions. You can become better and allow God to work through your suffering, or you can become bitter, turn inward, and reject how God is using your trial to shape your soul. How have you dealt with suffering in the past? During times of suffering, do you use it as an opportunity for reflection and communion with God? Are you willing to allow God to shape you through suffering?

And we know that all things work together for good
to those who love God, to those who are
called according to His purpose.
Romans 8:28

PART IV

COMMUNICATING WELL IN THE ARENA

16

EFFECTIVELY COMMUNICATING
IN A POST-TRUTH WORLD

In 2016, *Oxford Dictionaries* declared "post-truth" the Word of the Year, defining post-truth as "relating to or denoting circumstances in which objective facts are less influential in shaping public opinion than appeals to emotion and personal belief."[1] In other words, emotions trump objective facts.

It's common to hear, "Well, that's your truth," or "This is my truth." These phrases are a conversation stopper. They are also shallow. There are universal truths that apply to all of us, whether we believe them or not. For example, gravity is in full force in every part of the world every second of the day. And no matter how much you disbelieve in gravity, if you jump off a tall building thinking you can fly, you will come crashing down and be hurt very badly or die. Yet real harm to post-truth adherents is increasingly evident, especially to those embracing gender dysphoria and mutilating otherwise healthy organs.

For those who disbelieve in gravity, we should tell them that it's real and they may hurt themselves if they try to defy it.

Likewise, we should warn people whose gender dysphoria tells them to change their external appearance to conform to their mental state. People need to hear that there are consequences to gender transition, including a higher likelihood of suicide ideation or suicide attempts after sex mutilation surgery.

It's clear that we have lost a shared moral reference point. There is no up or down and no agreed-upon right or wrong in this post-truth age. We ought to try to reason with opponents of the gospel, but since we cannot reliably appeal to reason and objectivity in conversation, we must resort to a better story. Jesus reasoned with the Pharisees. He also told stories with deep truths that resonate in the heart.

Reflection: What is your story and how can you share it in a way that connects with others? Do you know how to relate to a post-Christian world? Do you know what the Lord would have you to do to bring gospel truths to a world in desperate need? Are you motivated by the well-being of your neighbors and the good of your community?

The tongue of the righteous is choice silver; the heart of the wicked is of little worth. The lips of the righteous feed many, but fools die for lack of sense.
Proverbs 10:20–21

Righteous lips are the delight of a king, and he loves him who speaks what is right.
Proverbs 16:13

What are you aiming to say?

A biologist, a chemist, and a statistician are out hunting. The biologist shoots at a deer and misses five feet to the left. The chemist takes a shot and misses five feet to the right. The statistician yells, "We got 'em!"

Sometimes we can be wide to the right or wide to the left in our words and think they balance out when we hit our target. But they don't.

It's so important that we're precise and careful when we communicate. A word five feet to the right or left is going to miss the mark, leaving the listener confused or, worse yet, the gospel misrepresented. Christ-followers should be grounded in basic Christian doctrine. This begins with submitting to and living according to God's Word, which is our starting point and the final word on Christian conduct. This includes how we communicate.

Colossians 4:6 is a great starting point. It says, "Let your conversation always be gracious, seasoned with salt, so that you may know how you ought to answer each person." Another important passage speaking to this topic is James 1:19–20, where we're told to be "quick to hear, slow to speak, slow to anger; for the anger of man does not produce the righteousness of God." There's a lot of anger today, isn't there? Both sides of the political spectrum are angry. But James tells us to be slow to anger. We're told to be slow to speak as well.

Reflection: What is preventing you from heeding James's admonition? Is the media you're consuming boiling your blood and making you angry? Are political pundits influencing you more than God's Word? Have you considered taking a media fast and spending that time of solitude in the Gospels, closely observing how Jesus engaged people?

Let no corrupting talk come out of your mouths, but only such as is good for building up, as fits the occasion, that it may give grace to those who hear.
Ephesians 4:29

17

WIN THE PERSON INSTEAD
OF THE ARGUMENT

I was a guest on the "Eastern Standard," an hour-long live radio show on Kentucky's widest-reaching public radio station, WEKU. John Hingsbergen hosted the lively conversation over President Trump's order to prohibit transgender soldiers in the military. Across the table were two transgender individuals: a man who identified as a woman and went by the name Tuesday and a woman who identified as a man. The other guest didn't show up, leaving me the lone conservative voice in the discussion.

After my adrenaline subsided, I settled in, looked across the table, and wondered what happened in their lives that led them to be so uncomfortable with their born sex that they would be compelled to live as the opposite sex. What kind of family did they come from? Did they suffer abuse? What was their story?

Call-in portions of any live program are wildcards. You never know what someone might say. "Christianity is about tolerance and love. It's not about judging others," the young seminary student chimed in during the call-in segment. "We should support our trans brothers and sisters and not put them down."

I responded that in my understanding of orthodox Christianity, God created the world. "He put the sun, moon, and stars in place. He created each of us in his image," I said. "But we rebelled against the Creator in Eden, and as a result, we live in a fallen, broken world. Jesus came nearly 2000 years ago to set us free from sin and put us in right relationship with God. Someday He's coming again to restore all things, and this is the good news of the gospel." Opportunities to share the gospel arise when you least expect them.

It's that same worldview that prompted me to treat my transgender opponents with dignity and respect. "Tuesday, I disagree with you on the issue of transgender identity and whether it's good, but that doesn't mean that I hate you," I told the man who identified and dressed as a woman across the table from me. "It means that I have a different opinion."

I realized at the time that the widespread acceptance of transgender identity had changed traditional modes of argumentation. Logic won't win the day in a post-truth age. We must tell a better story, and we must do it with love and compassion. Wasn't it God's love and compassion that paved the way for the gospel of Jesus to change our lives? We might not all be struggling with gender dysphoria, but the same gospel that radically altered our hard hearts has the power to transform the gender-confused person's heart as well.

Reflection: When you debate a political opponent, is your goal to crush them? Are you willing to lead conversations with grace? If you were debating a transgender activist, would you rather win the debate or win over the person? Do you have confidence that the gospel, graciously delivered, can change a life?

Do not be conformed to this world, but be transformed by the renewal of your mind, that by testing you may discern what is the will of God, what is good and acceptable and perfect.
Romans 12:2

19
_____

CONTRIBUTING TO BETTER
CONVERSATIONS

As a matter of good citizenship, every one of us is responsible for contributing positively to our society. When it comes to conversations, a few important principles come to mind. For starters, think the best of others. Do not begin the conversation looking down at them. Instead, see the person you're speaking with as a fellow image-bearer.

If the person holds positions or beliefs different than you, try to truly understand them. It's a good practice to restate what they're saying as you understand it. Then, ask them if that's what they mean. This shows respect. If you're tempted to criticize, don't. That's a conversation-stopper.

If you're prone to making snap judgments on someone you disagree with or who doesn't meet your standards, try to understand them. Ask them about their story, their family, and formative experiences. Try to be sympathetic. Instead of contributing to division, become a reconciler. After all, Jesus says, "Blessed are the peacemakers" (Matthew 5:9). Scripture also says, "As far as it depends on you, live at peace with everyone" (Romans 12:18 NIV).

If your community is in need of more peace, love, and mercy, let it start with you. Bring grace to the conversations you have with your family members, co-workers, and neighbors. We cannot wait for Hollywood or Top 40 radio to change the conversations. Better conversations will not come from a legislative act or executive order, nor will they come through the institutional news media. Instead, important change will happen through people just like you engaging others with lots of love.

Reflection: Is there room for improvement in conversations you have with political opponents? How about discussions on social media platforms? Has anyone ever asked why you are calm and kind when engaging in difficult conversations? In what ways can you contribute to better conversations?

Do not speak evil against one another, brothers. The one who speaks against a brother or judges his brother, speaks evil against the law and judges the law. But if you judge the law, you are not a doer of the law but a judge. There is only one lawgiver and judge, he who is able to save and to destroy. But who are you to judge your neighbor?
James 4:11–12

20

COMMUNICATING WITH ELECTED OFFICIALS

Have you ever wondered how to effectively communicate with public officials? It may seem intimidating, but it's not as threatening as you might think. For starters, you need to know who they are. If you don't already know your local leaders, get to know them. Local officials like city council members and state representatives are all fairly easy to connect with. Most are very interested in hearing from their constituents. By the way, you have more influence with them than with national leaders like US Representatives and Senators, and your local leaders can practically do more for your neighborhood and community than any leaders in Washington.

Here are a few pointers when communicating with elected officials.

Understand the roles and responsibilities of various officeholders. Know something about your elected officials and what their positions entail. Know the difference between a mayor and a member of Congress. Consider that a mayor cannot introduce a bill in Congress, and a senator can't put up a traffic signal on your road. You'll save yourself some time if you figure out who can best help resolve the issue.

Be respectful of their time. You're likely to bump into local elected officials at a local restaurant or in the grocery store. If what you have to say is longer than a minute, set up a time to speak with them in their office. If you do that, come prepared. Know the issue, know what you want to convey, and let them know what you'd like them to do.

Be careful with your tone. There is no quicker way to end the conversation and cut off your possibility of influence than to be rude or disrespectful. Colossians 4:6 bears repeating: "Let your conversation be always full of grace, seasoned with salt, so that you may know how to answer everyone" (NIV). The official may not share your political views and may not tell you what you want to hear, but you should always be respectful and gracious. There is no downside to grace.

Give honor where honor is due. If your elected leader is doing a good job, then tell them! Leaders are often told that they're doing something wrong or how pathetic they are, so it's refreshing to them when they hear, "Good job!" It's especially important if that leader is of another political persuasion and does a good job. This builds goodwill. It also builds a bridge to more opportunities in the future.

Exercise caution with respect to social media. In general, avoid sharing your thoughts about elected leaders on social media, especially if your thoughts are negative. If you wouldn't say something about a person to their face, why would you want to say it on a platform for the whole world to see? Before you post something, ask yourself: How are my comments going to help? Would my comments possibly hurt my cause? Could they hurt my credibility? How about my

Christian witness? More often than not, when it comes to commenting on political leaders, social media is not your friend.

Reflection: Have you ever had a conversation with an elected official? Consider praying for your elected leaders, and let them know you are praying for them. When you communicate respectfully and honorably, you garner their attention, and they will be more likely to listen to you.

Pay to all what is owed to them: taxes to whom taxes are owed, revenue to whom revenue is owed, respect to whom respect is owed, honor to whom honor is owed.
Romans 13:7

21

A RESPECTFUL APPROACH YIELDS FUTURE DIVIDENDS

O ne notable experience with a top legislative leader in Kentucky occurred during the 2021 legislative session. Earlier in the session, I was heavily engaged in the effort to stop the expansion of casino-style gambling, dubbed "Historical Horse Racing." The CPC team held virtual public forums, legislative briefings, and Facebook Live interviews and lobbied and provided talking points to legislators. We worked hard, but in the end, we unfortunately lost that battle.

Shortly after, we pivoted to another hot issue of school choice. A friend involved with the issue suggested I call one of the top leaders in the state House. I connected with him, and before we got far into the discussion, he said, "Richard, I know we were on opposite sides of an issue you felt strongly about and worked hard on, but I'd like to commend you for how you conducted yourself." I didn't expect to hear that, but it was an honor to hear those words.

We ended up having a good conversation and planned to work together on an issue we both agreed on. And we ended up winning. Some would say, "Nelson, you won one, and you lost one." But really, it was two wins. It's a win when you can respectfully engage an issue and when your former opponent sees grace in your actions. It's another win—and a much more important victory—when Christians represent King Jesus well. After all, we are Christ's ambassadors.

Reflection: Do you take the long view when approaching political issues? Does your conduct lead to ending relationships or building bridges? Do you carefully work to minimize animus? Have you asked God to work in seemingly impossible situations?

~

When a man's ways please the LORD,
he makes even his enemies to be
at peace with him.
Proverbs 16:7

22

SPEAKING EFFECTIVELY
IN PUBLIC MEETINGS

"The fire and sulfur coming down from the sky was ten thousand degrees and melted everything it touched." A friend in attendance relayed to me what the speaker told the city council. A dozen local leaders in this south-central Kentucky city were considering an ordinance that made LGBTQ+ identity a protected right. "Sodom was destroyed because of homosexuality, and we cannot be for something that God is against."

While the theological conviction is true that homosexual behavior is sinful and judged by God, too many well-intended believers try to deliver a sermonette in the public arena. A city council meeting is not a church service. Too many quote the Bible to an audience that doesn't value its authority. Scripture warns against "cast[ing]your pearls before swine" (Matthew 7:6 NKJV). In other words, don't share precious things with those who will likely trample them.

The prophet Isaiah said, "Come now, let us reason together" (1:18). Scripture also says to "let your reasonableness be known to everyone" (Philippians 4:5). It is biblical for

Christians to appeal to reason. Christians should be reasonable people. And when it comes to LGBTQ+ rights ordinances, there are perfectly reasonable arguments against them. Widely accepted public policy principles are often more effective in advancing your cause than solely quoting Scripture. For example, when debating sexually oriented businesses, an appeal to preserve the health, safety, and welfare of the community will likely get more traction than quoting a Bible verse. Consider that a reasonable approach and the right tone are effective and will likely win over elected leaders.

Speaking at Public Forums

If you plan to speak at a public meeting, research the topic and carefully plan your comments. Before you speak publicly, ask elected leaders for their understanding of the issue. Most will be happy to help. Prepare written comments before the meeting and run them by a trusted friend. If you plan to speak with a group, collaborate in advance so you don't repeat points others in your group plan to make.

Often, there's a sign-in process for those intending to speak. Make sure you register. Find out the allotted time for each speaker. It's usually around three minutes. Always respect the stated time limit. When it's your turn to speak, announce your name before speaking, then acknowledge and honor the elected body and the official presiding over the meeting. Thank them for the opportunity to speak.

Follow the 4 Bs: Be accurate. Be concise. Be gracious. Be brief. Also, don't ever ridicule the opposition, accuse public officials, be disrespectful, use inflammatory language, or cheer or clap after comments unless invited to do so by the one presiding over the meeting. Finally, it's okay not to speak. Not everyone needs to speak publicly, and sometimes, speaking publicly hurts your cause rather than helps.

Reflection: Have you ever spoken at a public meeting? Are you willing to be counseled by others? Are you willing to put these principles into practice the next time you speak at a public meeting?

When words are many, transgression is not lacking,
but whoever restrains his lips is prudent.
The tongue of the righteous is choice silver;
the heart of the wicked is of little worth.
The lips of the righteous feed many,
but fools die for lack of sense.
Proverbs 10:19–21

PART V

THE CHURCH AND THE POLITICAL REALM

"If we will not be governed by God, we must
be governed by tyrants."
—*Attributed to William Penn*

23

SHOULD PASTORS SPEAK
TO MORAL ISSUES?

I was invited to speak to a large church in Franklin, just south of Bowling Green, on the topic of Christianity and Culture. I addressed several current moral and social issues and challenged the church to think and engage biblically. For some reason, in the middle of my message, I paused and said, "Some of you might think this is political, but I've not mentioned any political party. Nor have I told you how to vote or who to vote for. These are moral issues, and God's Word speaks to these issues. We must process the issues through a biblical grid." I made the case that we must understand our role as a church in society and respond in a way that honors God.

After the service, I collected a sheet circulated during the meeting, where attendees could sign up for email updates. Someone had written at the top, in all caps: THIS IS PARTISAN POLITICAL PROPAGANDA AND HAS NO PLACE IN THE CHURCH. I couldn't help but think those words were being written the moment I added the footnote to the message.

Whether pastors should speak to moral and social issues depends on your view of God and the Bible. If you view God as sovereign and believe that the Bible speaks to all areas of life and culture, then speaking to moral and social issues is an outflow of that belief. Jesus claims "all authority in heaven and on earth" (Matthew 28:18). This means that Jesus has absolute authority over spiritual things and earthly things. The Lordship of Christ extends to all creation, and His followers owe Him total allegiance in all parts of life—not just their spiritual lives but their home, work, and civic lives.

Acknowledging the Lordship of Christ got the disciples punished and excommunicated by the Pharisees. It got the early church in trouble with Caesar. In the twentieth century, it put the Confessing Church in Germany in the crosshairs of the Nazi party. True belief in Jesus always has public implications, including political implications.

Abortion and sexual ethics—two of the hottest topics today—affect real people in the pews. When congregants make poor moral choices and suffer the consequences of those choices, pastors are expected to pick up the pieces. Since this is the case, why should a pastor's voice be restricted from speaking to public policies related to these issues? Are they doing the congregation any favors by remaining silent about injustice and evil authorized by the government? Sometimes, it takes grave government-sponsored evil like the Holocaust to wake the church. This is what moved Dietrich Bonhoeffer to start the Confessing Church movement.

Besides standing against unrighteousness (Psalm 94:16), the church contributes to healing people and culture (James 1:27). Throughout history, when Christians saw homeless children, they started orphanages. When they saw widows in distress, they provided help. When they saw the sick needing special help, they started hospitals. When they saw young minds that needed to be developed, they started universities. Dutch statesman Abraham Kuyper understood the Lordship of Christ, famously saying, "There is not a square inch in the whole domain of our human existence over which Christ, who is Sovereign over all, does not cry: 'Mine!'"[1] Do you believe this?

Reflection: If you're a pastor or ministry leader, are you discipling your congregation to think biblically about the great moral and social issues of the day? If not, why?

*All Scripture is breathed out by God and profitable for teaching,
for reproof, for correction, and for training in righteousness,
that the man of God may be complete,
equipped for every good work.
2 Timothy 3:16–17*

*Can wicked rulers be allied with you, those who frame injustice
by statute? They band together against the life of the righteous
and condemn the innocent to death. But the Lord has become
my stronghold, and my God the rock of my refuge. He will bring
back on them their iniquity and wipe them out for their
wickedness; the LORD our God will wipe them out.
Psalm 94:20–23*

24

EARTHLY POWER AND
ULTIMATE POWER

The LORD has established his throne in the heavens,
and his kingdom rules over all.
Psalm 103:19

In his book *The Long Game*, Senate Minority Leader Mitch McConnell said that "a political party is not a church."[1] This is true. Regardless of whether he meant to keep faith out of his political party, most of Sen. McConnell's political party are involved in church. Biblical values inform many Republicans (and those of other political affiliations) concerning how to think about the world and the great issues of the day.

Just as a political party is not a church, political leaders are not the church's deliverance from an unjust society. Even though political leaders have a place and a platform to promote righteous policies, their jurisdiction cannot reach the deepest problems that ail us—those found within the realm of the human heart. For society to change, there must be spiritual change in the individuals comprising society. Of course, this falls into the realm of the church. God's Word speaks to our true spiritual condition and describes the remedy to what ails us and what we ought to live for. No politician can teach this or legislate this. Nor should they. It should be clear that the problems we face in this nation are so much deeper and far beyond what any political leader could ever address.

There's something in every human heart that longs for things to be made right again, for everything that is now sad to someday be made untrue. It's a great temptation of politics to implement a vision of God's kingdom. It's easy in a secular age to believe that government can deliver whatever human need is lacking. It's a temptation that must be resisted because it implies that government can address all of life. But it cannot. The government might give out food to nourish the body, but it cannot give spiritual sustenance to the soul. It might provide a roof over one's head, but it cannot make a home. It might create a job, but it cannot fulfill one's calling. It might provide for any of the physical necessities of life, but one thing the government cannot do is give hope. Only God can do that.

The biblical worldview teaches that there is a King, and he doesn't reside at 1600 Pennsylvania Avenue or in the Senate Majority Leader's office. Scripture teaches that people have deep needs that cannot be addressed through legislation. As much as politicians try to solve current social dilemmas, they should never deliver a vision of the kingdom of God. Although they've tried, it's abundantly clear that the US Congress often falls far short of delivering coherent policy, much less God's kingdom.

Our modern American age is tempered by secularism and girded by material wealth. In our man-centered, pull-yourself-up-by-the-bootstraps approach to problem-solving, there's little need for God—even in the church. Perhaps this is why so many self-identified evangelicals put inordinate weight on a presidential election to restore the nation. It's not that the presidency isn't important or that it doesn't carry incredible influence over society. However, it is dangerous for Christians to neglect the biblical hope found only in Christ and disregard principles of conduct in order to get their candidate elected at any cost. Perhaps there's no greater crucible where faith will be tested than in the political realm. Wasn't this true for Moses, Daniel, Shadrach, Meshach, Abednego, and Esther? The temptation for believers to seek deliverance from temporary political leaders is a seduction the church has faced since ancient times.

Reflection: Is your ultimate hope evident in how you engage in the political realm? What would the world look like if Christians began to live out the ethics of Jesus publicly? How would it impact our corrosive politics? What would society look like if believers in business, education, media, and the arts and sciences pursued their professions according to kingdom values?

But in your hearts honor Christ the Lord as holy, always being
prepared to make a defense to anyone who asks you
for a reason for the hope that is in you;
yet do it with gentleness and respect.
1 Peter 3:15

25

SHOULD PASTORS ENDORSE POLITICAL CANDIDATES?

In 2019, the Associated Press reported that former Kentucky Governor Matt Bevin "urged a group of preachers to embrace political speech in the pulpit by telling them not to fear a federal law that prohibits candidate endorsements by tax-exempt churches."[1] Bevin called the law a "paper tiger." A leaked video made its way into the hands of the news media, who didn't like what they saw and heard.

I was very aware of the prayer event for pastors since I attended. In fact, I helped organize it. Pastors from across the Bluegrass packed out the Governor's Mansion, prayed for the governor, and heard him speak. Gov. Bevin said, "It's not about R's or D's; it's about what's right." He didn't tell them to endorse candidates or get their people to vote for a particular party. He urged them to work to restore a moral compass in a day when gender is no longer fixed and girls' restrooms, locker rooms, and team sports in our public schools are now open to biological males.

Should a pastor endorse political candidates? Even if a pastor endorses a candidate from the pulpit, should it be of any concern to a politician in Washington? It may be unwise for spiritual shepherds to get mired in the fray of petty power grabs, but it is not unconstitutional. If anything, the First Amendment protects the rights of pastors to preach unfettered messages without intrusion by the federal government. Churches can deal with the wisdom of whether a pastor should address politics and endorse candidates.

One concern, however, is that it's a pastor's job to protect the pulpit from becoming a tool for a political party. Another concern is when the government encroaches into church affairs and restricts messages from the pulpit.

Those who appear threatened by the church's engaging in cultural and political issues point to the Johnson Amendment, passed in 1954 by Texas Senator Lyndon B. Johnson. It was intended to muzzle his political opponents. The result is Section 501(c)3, barring "religious, charitable, scientific, . . . [or] literary [organizations] from participat[ing] in, or interven[ing] in (including the publishing or distributing of statements), any political campaign on behalf of (or in opposition to) any candidate for public office."[2] The measure wasn't originally meant to bar churches from commenting on candidates or speaking about social issues. And to date, only one church has ever lost its 501c3 tax status under the IRS code.

Maybe we're dealing with contentious social issues and the brokenness evident in so many lives because the pulpits have been silent too long. Intimidation and fear, some of it self-induced, have brought us to this point. If ever there's been a time for pastors to speak with clarity and boldness, it's now. If ever we needed more voices speaking to the need for moral reformation, it's now. After all, politicians don't have a monopoly on talking about these things.

When citizens adhere to a moral code prescribed by our Creator God, the nation's democratic institutions are more secure, society is more stable, and people have a chance to flourish. The father of our nation, George Washington, thought so and reminded us in his Farewell Address that "of all the dispositions and habits which lead to political prosperity, religion and morality are indispensable supports."[3] Gov. Bevin said essentially the same at the gathering of pastors in 2019.

Reflection: Have you asked your pastor how you can pray for him? Do you pray that God would grant him wisdom and courage to teach the Word as it applies to culture and the political realm? If the climate inside the church gets hot around the political season, do you seek to bring biblical clarity and peace to the situation or issues?

Therefore, as you received Christ Jesus the Lord, so walk in him,
rooted and built up in him and established in the faith, just as
you were taught, abounding in thanksgiving. See to it that no
one takes you captive by philosophy and empty deceit,
according to human tradition, according to the elemental
spirits of the world, and not according to Christ.
For in him the whole fullness of deity dwells bodily,
and you have been filled in him, who is the head
of all rule and authority.
Colossians 2:6–10

26

WHEN PASTORS BECOME PARTISAN

In a sermon delivered on May 15, 2022, Greg Locke, pastor of Global Vision Bible Church in Mt. Juliet, Tennessee, called Democrats demons and told them to get out. "You cannot be a Christian and vote Democrat in this nation. I don't care how mad that makes you. You can get as pissed off as you want to. You cannot be a Christian and vote Democrat in this nation. . . . You cannot be a Democrat and a Christian. You cannot. Somebody say, 'Amen.' The rest of you get out! Get out!"[1]

Kentucky also has pastors who resemble Greg Locke, confusing partisan affiliation with godliness. "You cannot be a registered Democrat and a Christian." The speaker's voice boomed throughout the Eastern Kentucky pavilion at a pre-election gathering in 2016. "You cannot vote Democrat and be a Christian. Democrats are for abortion, for homosexual marriage, and anti-God." Several pastors, elected officials, and local citizens listened to the tirade. I cringed inside, not because of the policy positions identified as antithetical to Scripture but because of the harsh tone. Condemnation and anger bordered on rage. Where was grace and kindness? Where was the sensitivity to the audience? Wherever it was, it was clear there was little room for the fruit of the Spirit.

What about the new Christian who was still a registered Democrat? What about the nonpolitical person who hadn't given much thought to political affiliation? What about Democratic officeholders who were capable public servants, held Christian values, and governed accordingly? The speaker's condemnation overpowered any of these considerations.

A great threat to the purity of the church is that Christian orthodoxy has become subservient to political identity. The self-appointed partisan gatekeepers in the church and their political litmus tests say that if one believes the wrong thing about a candidate or their politics, then one must not be a Christian. Greg Locke's fiery condemnation wasn't addressing sin against a holy God; it was a condemnation of people with the wrong political identity. Christianity teaches that the new spiritual identity of a Christ-follower is preeminent and shapes their politics, not the other way around.

Rank-and-file Christians sometimes allow their political exuberance to dominate them. Such has been the case in recent years. "We're voting with our middle finger," the South Carolina voter told the two reporters from the *Los Angeles Times*.[2] This was before the state's 2016 Republican primary. The reporters tried to get a pulse on the evangelical vote, the largest significant voting bloc in the South Carolina primary, and the image of an evangelical's middle finger was incongruent with Christian principles. After all, the mark of a Christ-follower isn't how one feels politically but rather "if you have love for one another" (John 13:35).

There is a clear and present danger when Christ's followers are identified more by their political allegiance than loyalty to their Savior. It's more than problematic when a Christian's politics become all-consuming and combative; it's repulsive.

The same is true today when Christian leaders give more credence to political parties and candidates than they deserve. On the one hand, pastors should not be afraid to speak about the social and moral issues of the day. On the other hand, they should closely guard the pulpit from being commandeered by any political party or politician who would use it for political gain. Christians ought to realize that no political party will deliver the kingdom. Only Christ the King can do that.

Reflection: Does your love for your fellow brothers and sisters in the body of Christ outweigh your political opinions? If your political allegiance has damaged relationships in the church, how will you go about repairing the rupture?

And the Lord's servant must be kind to everyone, able to teach,
patiently enduring evil, correcting his
opponents with gentleness.
2 Timothy 2:24–25

27

SIX OBJECTIONS TO CHRISTIAN POLITICAL ENGAGEMENT

Can you legislate morality?

I briefed the Franklin County Judge-Executive on a model ordinance that restricted sexually oriented businesses (SOBs), a fitting acronym for businesses that objectify and exploit women. A magistrate also joined the meeting, and both agreed that the county residents would be well-served with regulations intended to minimize harm from SOBs. The judge set up another meeting with the county attorney. I briefed the attorney about the vulnerability of the county and the model ordinance we would provide to save him the work of drafting a new one from scratch. Unfortunately, he wasn't convinced it was worth his time. "I'm dealing with child abuse cases, trying to get deadbeat dads to pay child support, and we have a drug crisis on our hands," he said. "And you want me to inspect strip clubs? I'm not wasting my time with that." The attorney stood up and abruptly left the meeting. As the door closed, the county judge apologized to me.

The Franklin County Attorney implied that I was imposing my moral views on the county and that he had no time for it. We've all heard it before: "Stop imposing your morality." But the problem is that the person who says this is imposing their own moral sense. We all have moral views, including elected officials. And all laws are based on a moral view. The question is, which moral view will prevail?

In my view, women are not objects of exploitation, and to preserve the health, safety, and welfare of a community, SOBs should be restricted. Nearly every county government I reached unanimously agreed. Through persuasion and scores of presentations to local governments—and at other times quietly behind the scenes—between 2004 and 2008, I was able to directly and indirectly help 116 Kentucky counties enact ordinances that restricted strip clubs and other SOBs from exploiting women.

"Jesus wasn't political."

Another common objection to Christian engagement in politics is that Jesus wasn't political. Some even contend, like Minnesota pastor Greg Boyd, that all civil government is "demonic." Boyd's influential book *The Myth of a Christian Nation* bases his assertion on Satan's statement to Jesus when he showed Jesus the kingdoms of the world and promised to give them to Jesus if he'd only bow down and worship him (Luke 4).[1]

We know that Satan is a liar and the father of lies. The kingdoms of the world are not his to give. One of the most poignant political statements of Jesus's power and authority was when he stood silently before Pilate, facing unjust and false charges. Pilate became angry and said, "You will not speak to me? Do you not know that I have authority to release you and authority to crucify you?" Jesus's response was direct: "You would have no authority over me at all unless it had been given you from above. Therefore he who delivered me over to you has the greater sin" (John 19:10–11).

Pilate had no authority except that God had put him in power. Scripture speaks of government as an institution ordained by God. Romans 13:1–6 makes this clear:

> Let every person be subject to the governing authorities. For there is no authority except from God, and those that exist have been instituted by God. . . . For rulers are not a terror to good conduct, but to bad. Would you have no fear of the one who is in authority? Then do what is good, and you will receive his approval, for he is God's servant for your good . . . for the authorities are the ministers of God.

This passage makes clear that civil government is God's idea. Those in power have an obligation to uphold the common good and punish wrongdoers (even though this hasn't always been the case throughout history). Christians have an obligation to abide by the law, be good citizens, and see government service as a legitimate vocation.

Vestiges of a biblical worldview in the West are found in several European nations that have high offices called ministries. Germany has the Ministry of Defense, and England has the Ministry of Justice. This idea stems from the Reformational understanding of God instituting government to be a minister for His glory and the good of the people. Even though the West has jettisoned a biblical worldview, government is still in place for God's glory and for His people to engage.

∾

The Most High rules the kingdom of men and gives it to whom he will and sets over it the lowliest of men.
Daniel 4:17b

Isn't our citizenship in heaven?

Some argue that Christians shouldn't be involved in government and point to Paul's statement to the Philippians: "But our citizenship is in heaven, and from it we await a Savior, the Lord Jesus Christ" (Philippians 3:20). Paul reminds the church that their ultimate citizenship is in heaven and their ultimate allegiance is to Christ. This does not mean that earthly citizenship does not matter. In Romans 13:6–7, Paul tells the church to "give to everyone what you owe them," including paying taxes and paying respect. Jesus also commands His followers to render to Caesar what is Caesar's (Matthew 22:21). This includes honoring citizenship responsibilities like paying taxes.

Practically, Christians have dual citizenship. If you were born in the United States, you are automatically a US citizen. If you were born in Kentucky, you are a native Kentucky citizen. As a citizen, you have obligations. Paying taxes, voting, and participating in your community are a few citizenship duties. Fulfilling these duties is part of practically loving your neighbor.

Throughout Scripture, we see several examples of God's people engaging in government. In fact, there are two main categories of heroes in the Old Testament: prophets and political leaders. Sometimes, their roles overlapped. Joseph served as second only to Pharaoh in Egypt. Daniel counseled and served four different pagan kings in Babylon and Persia. Esther, Moses, and David were also political leaders used by God.

Christians who believe in the Lordship of Christ cannot but be good citizens in this earthly realm. In fact, they ought to be the best citizens, unselfishly involved as they're able, even involving themselves with politics at some level. Christians must engage politically either through voting, helping good candidates get elected, or running for office themselves. The good of their neighbor and the good of the community is at stake. If God's Word speaks to all of life and culture, then why would believers shun a platform of influence where these principles could be lived out through Christian leadership? If God's principles speak to righteousness and justice, then why shouldn't Christians bring their perspective to government?

Can you change a heart through the law?

Opponents of civil rights leaders in the 1950s and 1960s often argued that the heart of a racist could not be changed through the law. To this, Martin Luther King Jr. responded, "It may be true that the law cannot make a man love me, religion and education will have to do that, but it can restrain him from lynching me. And I think that's pretty important also."[2]

The purpose of the law was never meant to change hearts. Only God can do that. The function of the law is to restrain evil. The law implicitly protects human rights: life, liberty, and property. It prohibits certain activities and imposes consequences on those who do wrong. It may be said that the law is about telling society what is expected and using force to stop someone from imposing their immorality on somebody else.

What about the separation of church and state?

"Well, I'm a Baptist, and my faith tradition teaches there's a separation of church and state," the State Supreme Court Justice representing the 1st Judicial District at the time told me and a colleague. It was a chance meeting; as we were walking through the capitol, we crossed paths with the distinguished justice, who invited us into his office and gave us a brief tour of the courtroom. He continued, "I believe it's necessary for the good of the church to stay out of politics." His comment, not meant to be confrontational, came up during our conversation when I told him about CPC's work with churches to help them think about politics biblically and engage the culture appropriately.

The most common objection leveled at Christians seeking to influence the law and culture concerns "separation of church/state." Many mistakenly assert that the First Amendment to the US Constitution says something about "separation" or "separating church and state." It does not. It says, "Congress shall make no law respecting an establishment of religion, or prohibiting the free exercise thereof." This is a restriction on Congress—not a restriction on churches or individuals. It wasn't even understood at the time of its writing to be a restriction on states. In fact, there were state-sponsored churches until the early nineteenth century.[3]

The phrase "separation of church and state" can be traced to a letter Thomas Jefferson sent to a group of Baptists in Danbury, Connecticut. The Danbury Baptists were concerned about the state restricting religious freedom and meddling in church affairs. At the time, there were state government-sponsored churches, and minority denominations like the Baptists were deeply concerned about unfavorable treatment from the government. To their relief, Jefferson assured them that the First Amendment "erects a wall of separation" protecting them from the federal government infringing on religious freedom.[4]

Followers of Jesus who take the Lordship of Christ seriously see government as under God's rule. To the believer, God is Lord of the church and Lord of the state. Followers who take Jesus at His word cannot but pray for, engage, and influence government. This honors God and is for the good of others.

This does not mean that once in power, Christians can force their faith on the public through a law. This wrongly usurps the power of the Holy Spirit to bring someone to faith, and such power by the state would also violate conscience. Nor does this mean that Christians in public office can impose Christian doctrines on the population. For example, the law cannot compel church attendance (as did the Puritans) as a prerequisite to citizenship or holding office.

There are clearly two distinct realms of church and state. But they are not isolated. In fact, there is a nexus between the two. It may be said that the church deals in soul craft, or spiritual formation of individuals. The state, on the other hand, regulates how citizens should live with one another in community. The Declaration of Independence recognizes the nexus between what the church teaches, that there is a God who gives each of us rights, and the role of the state, which protects the inalienable God-given rights of its citizens.

A good society in which human rights are respected relies upon individuals embracing sound Christian doctrine and is tempered by sound Christian engagement. England's Lord John Fletcher Moulton said citizens in a good society adhere to "obedience to the unenforceable."[5] In other words, subjects must embrace a personal self-discipline that the law cannot force. This is an obligation to something higher and unseen. Virtue is the result. The teaching of virtues comes from the church. This is why the church should be considered an ally in the state's objective of keeping order and upholding human rights. When the church faithfully engages in the spiritual formation of its members, it inevitably creates good citizens, and this certainly makes the job of governing easier for the state.

There must be a healthy balance between the Christian community and the political realm. The church teaches the idea of human rights, moral restraints, and love of neighbor. The state protects individual rights and restrains immorality. Our second president, John Adams, understood this when he told the Massachusetts militia, "We have no government armed with power capable of contending with human passions unbridled by morality and religion. Our constitution was made for a moral and religious people. It is wholly inadequate to the government of any other."[6]

Both the church and the state operate under God's authority. Followers of Jesus must deliberately and carefully take the principles of the Christian faith into all of life, including the public and political realms.

"There are no absolutes."

"That may be your truth. But I'm living according to my truth" is a popular phrase today. We live in a time of moral relativism in which individuals define their own moral code, a time of little to no consensus on moral absolutes. This can be traced to Friedrich Nietzsche's philosophy, which did more to rattle the shared moral consensus of the West than anyone in his day. His revolutionary statement, "There are *no eternal facts*, as there are likewise no absolute truths,"[7] is being lived out today.

To say there are no absolutes is an absolute statement. Such a statement is godlike, implying that one is infinite in understanding and has the ultimate authority to make such a bold claim. For anyone to come on the scene and claim that there is no right or wrong and all actions are relative is the pinnacle of arrogance. One must ask upon *whose* authority is such a sweeping statement made?

One may believe there are no absolutes, just as they may believe they can fly like a bird and defy gravity. However, as soon as they jump off the tenth floor of a building, they are subject to gravity's domain and will suffer the effects of disobeying the law of gravity. No matter how much someone believes in something, it doesn't make it true. Truth is not relative. It is objective. Truth is also knowable. As the saying goes, "In a time of universal deceit, telling the truth is a revolutionary act." It's time to tell the truth.

Reflection: Have you ever been confronted with any of these objections? How have you addressed your critics? Do you see these objections as an opportunity to point critics to the reality of God?

For his invisible attributes, namely, his eternal power and divine nature, have been clearly perceived, ever since the creation of the world, in the things that have been made. So they are without excuse.
Romans 1:20

The danger of church/state entanglement

Even though Christians are called to live out their faith in society, it's important to recognize the danger of the church becoming politically entangled. The Roman Catholic Church's alignment with the state in the Middle Ages corrupted its moral authority. Likewise, the role of the state as the enforcer of church doctrine corrupted the role of the state. The corruption continued in the New World when Puritan New England restricted religious liberty by denomination and enacted civil punishment on unbelievers, the most egregious example being the Salem Witch Trials. This changed with the American Revolution and the new nation formed eleven years after the Declaration of Independence.

America's Founding Fathers realized that the roles of church and state are separate and should not be conflated. The government isn't responsible for evangelizing or overseeing the spiritual development of its citizens, nor should it subsidize churches or punish people for failing in their spiritual obligations to their Creator. The government is not a Sunday School teacher; however, when crimes are perpetrated against others, the state steps in.

The genius of the US Constitution is that it presupposes a higher law and source of rights above government without imposing a national religion or coercing individual beliefs. Indeed, Article VI forbids religious tests for federal officeholders.[8] However, the Constitution never required laws to be secular in origin or officeholders to check their most deeply held religious values at the door. What else would inform their conscience and behavior?

Implicit recognition of God and a higher law deftly made its way into our civil law without being overbearing or tyrannical. When the Constitutional Convention was on the verge of breaking down on June 28, 1787, a frail Benjamin Franklin arose and implored his fellow delegates to pray, just as they had done at the beginning of the Revolution:

> Our prayers, Sir, were heard, & they were graciously answered. . . . And have we now forgotten that powerful friend? or do we imagine that we no longer need his assistance? I have lived, Sir, a long time, and the longer I live, the more convincing proofs I see of this truth—that God Governs in the affairs of men. And if a sparrow cannot fall to the ground without his notice, is it probable that an empire can rise without his aid? We have been assured, Sir, in the sacred writings, that "except the Lord build the House they labour in vain that build it." I firmly believe this; and I also believe that without his concurring aid we shall succeed in this political building no better, than the Builders of Babel.[9]

That a fiercely independent people who separated from the world's greatest power after a long and costly war could come together and create such a magnificent document birthing a new federal government is incredible. That they refused to establish an official state religion without divorcing God from the government is a blessing.

∾

He changes times and seasons; he removes kings and sets up kings; he gives wisdom to the wise and knowledge to those who have understanding.
Daniel 2:21

28

LASTING CULTURAL CHANGE IS SPIRITUALLY LED

Followers of Jesus within the Roman Empire led radically distinct lives when they lived out the second Great Commandment to love their neighbor as themselves. They rescued infant girls left to die in the streets. They broke down socioeconomic, ethnic, and gender barriers as they welcomed women and enslaved people into their community. They broke bread together and cared for one another's needs. They were not politically powerful. In fact, they were powerless. They did not run for office. They couldn't. Nor did they issue press releases or policy positions. Something better was at work. Their lives were policy statements to a broken world in desperate need of a Savior. Their allegiance to another king was breathtaking. Their way of doing life was subversive, and their simple refusal to burn incense to Caesar cost many of them their very lives.

Rumors were spread about Christians, that they were cannibals and practiced incest. But it was their stubborn commitment to Christ that led some to be sentenced to death, sometimes dressed in animal skins and marched into the

Colosseum to be torn by wild beasts. Others were dipped in tar and hung on posts as torches to light Nero Caesar's roads so his guests could make their way to his feasts.

Would it have been easier for Christians to burn the incense to Caesar and keep their lives? Yes. But they were convinced that they were in God's hands. Their primary allegiance was to Jesus. After all, no Caesar ever overcame death and walked out of the grave. Such commitment to and love for the Living God and such acts of brotherly love and caring for the poor and needy won over the brutal, hedonistic status quo. In the early fourth century, Emperor Constantine legalized Christianity, and by the late fourth century, Christianity became the official religion of Rome under Emperor Theodosius I.

Just as Christians lived distinct lives in the first century, twenty-first-century Christians do the same today. The Christ-centered addiction recovery center called Isaiah House employs several hundred staff and serves thousands of Kentuckians annually. Cheri Scott directs Avenues for Women, a pregnancy care center in Frankfort that walks alongside women in crisis pregnancies. My friend and CPC board member Angela Minter leads Sisters for Life, a ministry that cares for women considering abortion. Dale Suttles directs Sunrise Children's Services, which provides a safe place for abused and neglected children and helps find safe, permanent homes for children living in foster care. These ministries don't often make headlines. The ministry leaders aren't usually listed in the Who's Who of Kentucky, but they're making a significant impact in the lives of real people every day.

The most profound life-changing work doesn't come from a powerbroker's office where the latest government policy is concocted. Nor does it come from cold hard cash. A person's deepest needs are met when compassion from another meets them where they are. And their motivation is otherworldly. Glimpses of the kingdom of God can be seen throughout the Commonwealth, and one day, the kingdom of God in its fullness will be experienced here on earth.

Reflection: Do you see yourself as a subject and citizen of God's kingdom? Have you considered using the gifts and talents the Lord has given you to expand His kingdom wherever you find yourself? Do you believe the King will someday return to restore all things and resume His rightful reign?

~

Then I saw "a new heaven and a new earth," for the first heaven and the first earth had passed away, and there was no longer any sea. I saw the Holy City, the new Jerusalem, coming down out of heaven from God, prepared as a bride beautifully dressed for her husband. And I heard a loud voice from the throne saying, "Look! God's dwelling place is now among the people, and he will dwell with them. They will be his people, and God himself will be with them and be their God. 'He will wipe every tear from their eyes. There will be no more death' or mourning or crying or pain, for the old order of things has passed away."
He who was seated on the throne said, "I am making everything new!" Then he said, "Write this down, for these words are trustworthy and true."
Revelation 21:1–5

PART VI

PLANNING YOUR
POLITICAL JOURNEY

29

ASK THE RIGHT QUESTIONS

Why are you running?

The voters will ask you why you are running for office. This requires a convincing and heartfelt answer. But you must first ask yourself: Why *are* you running for office? This will require some soul-searching and answering a myriad of questions honestly. Do you want to run for office because you have strong opinions about particular issues? Are you angry about the status quo? Does the current officeholder frustrate you? Do you want to serve your community? Do you bring in a skill set that enables you to serve well? Is your temperament conducive to successfully serving? Have others asked you to serve? Is the seat you're considering the best seat for you to serve in? Is it a calling on your life?

Are you of good character?

"Is there anything in your past that you wouldn't want to see on the front page of your local newspaper?" the interviewer asked the candidate running for governor. It's a question CPC's political advisory committee asks of every candidate we consider for endorsement. Be prepared with an honest answer. Good character is a priority value of CPC. This doesn't mean that candidates might not have made a past mistake or made poor choices at some point. In fact, several candidates we've endorsed have a past. They've owned their mistakes and are genuinely different people now. Owning mistakes is a sign of character. Charting a new path of good character is a sign of courage. Such a new course can merit an endorsement from the CPC.

Do you have the right temperament?

"If you could only choose one weapon to defeat your opponent," the political strategist asked the audience of aspiring political leaders, "would you choose a .22 or a nuclear bomb?" No, he wasn't advocating violence, but he was using a metaphor to make an important point. Conservative candidates from across the Commonwealth attended CPC's first candidate training event in 2013, and they wanted to know how to win. Attendees came from all walks of life and planned to run for offices ranging from city council to state Senate. What distinguished the winners from the losers was how they would ultimately answer the speaker's question. Their motivations and their temperament usually determined their electability.

Some see politics as the only way to save the country. It's a desperate war between good and evil, and it's about destroying the other side and keeping them from power. The nuclear bomb is often the first option for many hard-core conservatives. But have you considered that anyone with that mindset shouldn't be anywhere near the black box of nuclear controls?

Can you handle criticism?

Holding political office is not a normal job, nor is the way you get into office normal. Your resume—your entire life—is on display for all. The job interview is held in public. You'll have hundreds or even thousands of interviewers. Mistakes made along the way will eventually come to light. Mistakes made in public forums—whether on radio, TV, or in town hall meetings—become immediately known and broadcast to all.

It's not that mistakes cannot be overcome, but ask yourself these crucial questions: Are you able to take criticism? Are you able to overcome gaffes and take them in stride? Can you lighten up and laugh at yourself? Or will you be mortified by your blunders? As a candidate, you have an opportunity to shine. At the same time, any blemishes and imperfections will be on display. Running for political office may not be the best choice if you're overly sensitive and introspective.

Are you humble enough to be vulnerable with others?

The first step to any successful campaign is to seek wise counsel. Talk to your pastor and ask if he thinks you have the qualities to be a good leader. Ask your friends and trusted colleagues about what they see in you. If you are married, what does your spouse think of your leadership abilities? Is your spouse on board? If not, then running for office at that moment is not the best decision.

If you plan to serve in office, you will be giving counsel to others, but this first step—the ability to receive counsel—is an important test. If you cannot receive counsel from people who have your best interests in mind, then running for office is likely not for you.

The best counsel to seek is the Lord's. Is He calling you to run for office? How much time have you spent in prayer? Are you sensing His peace as you talk to Him about running? If you get the green light from family, friends, and, most importantly, God, then perhaps it's your time to run for office.

If you're not the one . . .

Just as every football team has one quarterback and every baseball team has one pitcher, every political candidate needs many team members to help them be successful. They need people to host fundraising events, volunteers to knock on doors and hand out campaign literature, phone bank volunteers, and donors. Successful candidates have a great team surrounding them and know how to motivate and lead their teams well.

Furthermore, political power is not the only way to make a difference in the culture. Culture building requires good leadership in government. It also requires layers of healthy leadership in other institutions, including schools, business, media, and the arts and sciences. Perhaps your calling and the most significant contribution you can make to a God-honoring culture is as a journalist, businessman, or teacher.

Reflection: Have you asked if you are best suited to be a political "quarterback"? Or are you best suited to play another role to help a better candidate? Are you willing to do other jobs to help a better candidate and "your team" down the field? Have you sought God's direction?

But select capable men from all the people—men who fear God, trustworthy men who hate dishonest gain—and appoint them as officials over thousands, hundreds, fifties and tens.
Exodus 18:21 NIV

30

KNOW WHEN TO RUN

T he Tea Party movement was in full stride in 2009 when I learned that the magistrate representing my area of the county would not run for re-election after serving one term. I was interested in the position, so I talked to Betty Sue Howard, head of the Republican Women's Club, and asked her about running. I also spoke with other key people in Trigg County politics, and they gave me the green light.

For years, I had encouraged conservative Christians to run for office. "We need principled leaders to run for office," I told group after group, year after year. After praying and talking it over with my family, I decided it was time to take my own advice and run for office.

Opportunities come in all shapes and sizes. Knowing when it's the right time and opportunity to run for office must be carefully considered. Prayer, family backing, and community support are vital. Miss any of those, and you may be chasing an illusion, not an opportunity. If those key supports fall into place, promptly moving ahead and deliberately executing a plan are essential.

When sizing up an opportunity in the political realm, you must understand your community. Know the key groups and their goals. Know the influencers. In Trigg County's 5th District, farmers were the key. Then, find your lane. Mine was mainly within the church community. I worked with pastors and churches throughout the area for years. I spoke at many of the churches, and the people knew me. Many also listened to me on the radio, where I had a weekly live morning program. It helps immensely when you're already engaged in the community and known by the public.

It's also important to understand the political temperament of voters. The voters in my district were very conservative. Even though around 65 percent were registered Democrats, they were fiscally and socially conservative. They were tired of high taxes, government regulation, and overspending, and they wanted a candidate who saw things their way. By all indications, I was their guy, even as a conservative Republican, and it appeared this was my opportunity to run for office.

Understanding your community, discerning the right moment to run, assessing the political temperament of voters, and knowing your lane are essential to running a successful race. Yet, there was something else at work in my decision to run for office. I believed I was being called to run. Everything appeared to confirm this. For the follower of Jesus, it's important to seek His face to discern calling. It's just as important to realize that the Lord is sovereign over who He places in office. With that in mind, regardless of the election results—win or lose—I needed to be content with the outcome.

Reflection: Have you pinpointed the best time for you to run for office? How will your decision affect your family? Will you be okay with the outcome, especially if you lose?

Look carefully then how you walk, not as unwise but as wise,
making the best use of the time, because the
days are evil. Therefore do not be foolish, but
understand what the will of the Lord is.
Ephesians 5:15–17

31

UNDERSTAND THE
POLITICAL LANDSCAPE

I t's always an advantage for a political candidate to be native to the district. My disadvantage in running for local office was that I was not a lifelong resident of Trigg County. I'd only been there for 12 years. My opponent, on the other hand, was a cradle Trigg Countian. His family had deep roots and was well respected. He was a fifth-generation family farmer and active in his church. He knew many more people and many more people knew him and his family better than they knew me—a transplant from the North. When I first moved to Kentucky, there was a language barrier. I spoke Wisconsinese, a dialect unfamiliar to most Kentuckians. Heck, I didn't know I had an accent until people kindly pointed it out with their Southern charm. "Yer not from 'round here son, are yeh?" Many thought I was a soldier at nearby Fort Campbell, home of the 101st Airborne Division.

My opponent for the 5th District Magistrate seat went to school with scores of Trigg Countians. He went to ballgames and community events and watched his classmates and neighbors' kids grow up. He knew the county's history.

Though I didn't have nearly as many friends or know the county's history, I made this work to my advantage. I approached every voter with a clean slate and no preconceived notions. I didn't know about the dumb things they did in high school or the trouble they got in with their neighbors or even the law. I was just the guy running for magistrate and asking every single one of them for their vote.

One point about local history when running for office is that ignorance is never a good thing. The more you know and understand, the better off you are. I'm not talking about gossip and slander. Those twin evils will waste your time and sap your focus faster than anything. Discerning the line between knowing essentials relevant to your campaign and garbage about people is a fine line. Be careful not to cross the line. As a rule, treat every voter with respect and kindness.

I testified before the Murray State University (MSU) Board of Regents on the controversial subject of sexual orientation and gender identity (SOGI). They were considering including LGBTQ+ identity as a new protected class in their employment policy, and I made the case that this was a bad idea. The Board of Regents was comprised of distinguished members from across the region, including a judge, successful businesspeople, and other pillars of the community. They all listened attentively but ultimately voted to amend MSU's hiring practices. They likely had their minds made up before I arrived.

John Archibald Wheeler, a theoretical physicist who worked with Albert Einstein, summarized his observations of Einstein's work by noting that "in the middle of every difficulty lies opportunity."[1] This maxim holds true when it comes to policy defeats and failure to persuade leaders and policymakers. I met with one of the Regents afterward, a successful engineer and philanthropist in Murray who appreciated and agreed with my presentation. He went on to tell a story about a man who crossed a deep creek without getting wet. Another man observed from a distance and said, "Mister, that creek was over your head, and yet you walked across it without getting wet." The man responded, "Come over here." As they walked back to the creek, he pointed to a tree stump just under the surface near the shore where he began his walk. Then he pointed to another one beyond that and another toward the middle. He said, "Look, so long as you know where the stumps are, you can walk on water."

Knowing people and the issues they care about are like figurative stumps. Knowledgeable people are key to getting things done. Whether a policy vote or a leadership election, you need help from the right people to persuade others. Knowing where the stumps are can make it look like you can walk on water, all the way to a policy win or elective office.

Reflection: Do you "know the stumps" in your local community? Do you have the temperament to approach the stumps carefully? Are you humble enough to tell the truth if voters think you can "walk on water"?

When you pass through the waters, I will be with you; and
through the rivers, they shall not overwhelm you; when
you walk through fire you shall not be burned,
and the flame shall not consume you.
Isaiah 43:2

32

MAKE LEMONADE OUT OF LEMONS

O ne thing is certain in any campaign: there will be difficulties. Your plans will go awry. People will disappoint you. Your party may abandon you. The opposition may misrepresent you. In the course of your campaign, you will be handed lemons. Too many people facing trouble leave the raw lemon in their mouths, and their contorted faces betray them. What will you do when given lemons?

The weather wasn't cooperating. A snow storm in the Cincinnati suburbs of Northern Kentucky dropped four inches of snow in the early morning hours, leaving the roads hazardous. A half dozen presenters were lined up to speak at our all-day candidate training. The phone rang at 7:00 a.m., less than two hours before the training was set to begin. Martin was on the other line, telling me he couldn't make it out of his driveway. He apologized for not being able to cover his session. He was the first of several presenters who would not be able to lead sessions at our candidate training event. Half the attendees arrived at the hotel before the storm hit, and calling off the event wasn't an option. I got on the phone with presenters who lived in the area, many of whom were state legislators and elected officials. I revamped the program, filled in the gaps, and pushed ahead. I explained to the attendees that the weather had handed us lemons: "This is what will happen to you on the campaign trail. And when you are handed lemons when you run for office, you need to make lemonade!"

Reflection: How have you dealt with botched plans? What have you learned about yourself when your plans fell through? Do you allow disappointments to grow your character?

∿

Many are the afflictions of the righteous, but
the LORD delivers him out of them all.
Psalm 34:19

33

AVOID NEGATIVE INFLUENCES

"Well, son, if you lie with dogs, you'll eventually get fleas," the elder statesman advised the aspiring politician. And in politics, the best way to avoid fleas is to stay away from places you can get them. The Kentucky state legislature found itself in the thick of proverbial fleas when a major scandal broke in 1996. According to *Courier-Journal* reporter Joe Gerth, influential Legislative Research Commission staffer Kent Downey "had a condom tree in his office and hookers and strippers on his payroll [and] was running X-rated golf scrambles out of the state House operations office."[1] Hardly the image of respect and honor people expect of their representatives.

Greg Stumbo, friends with Downey, eventually became Speaker of the House, and a culture of loose morals that disregarded sexual harassment continued under his leadership, tempting and eventually tainting other legislators along the way. Another sex scandal emerged in 2013, involving the reprimand of a few legislators and a $400,000 settlement with women who were sexually harassed while working for the Legislative Research Commission.[2] The scandals were one reason for the historic shift in power from Democrat to Republican in the 2016 state House elections.

You are known by the friends you keep. The friends and the company you keep will rub off on you with greater consequences than mere political affiliation. Republicans who keep the wrong friends and aspire to the wrong values can find themselves in the same snare as their Democratic rivals. Be watchful. Be on your guard. Draw clear lines to preserve your integrity. If you are not intentional, you are vulnerable to stumbling whether you're in public office or elsewhere.

What are your influences? Who are the friends you keep? Are they challenging you to grow in character and virtue? If you want to be like George Washington, spend time with people like John Adams. If your character and destiny don't mean much to you, then it doesn't matter who you hang with.

Reflection: Are you known by the company you keep? Are you careful when making friends?

∾

Do not be deceived: "Bad company ruins good morals."
1 Corinthians 15:33

∾

The headline at WUKY.org was devastating: "Kentucky House Speaker Jeff Hoover Resigns Leadership Post after Texts with Staffer."[3] It was November 5, 2017, less than a year after being elected the first Republican Speaker of the House in nearly 100 years. A dream of a lifetime dashed in seconds. All for what? A fleeting moment? A temporary lapse of judgment? In either case, the $110,000 nondisclosure settlement wasn't enough to protect the Speaker and two other colleagues caught up in the mess.

It takes years to get elected to high office, and it takes even longer to develop the solid relationships that land one in a place of high leadership. However, it only takes a moment to ruin everything. This is a recurring lesson in the political world: trust, credibility, and reputation with the public can be vaporized in a few moments of bad judgment. And it's clear that neither political party is immune to major scandals.

In 2000, Rep. Vance Wilkins and his Republican party won a majority in the Virginia House of Delegates. Within a year, he resigned his post after a similar scandal. Breaching the public's trust is the quickest way to burn political capital that took years to build.

Be on your guard. If you find yourself in a place of power and influence, guard your integrity like an Australian Shepherd guards a flock of sheep. There are deceiving and sinister forces that would like to tear your soul to bits and pieces. Rising to the top in any endeavor and leading any organization makes you a visible target. And you are not a target only for your enemies. Power and prominence also create an opportunity for your flesh and its untamed desires to have control.

Reflection: Do you avoid negative influences in your life? Do you guard your thoughts? Do you avoid situations that could compromise your integrity? Do you stay away from people who may lead you down the wrong path?

Be sober-minded; be watchful. Your adversary the devil prowls around like a roaring lion, seeking someone to devour.
1 Peter 5:8

Let no one say when he is tempted, "I am being tempted by God," for God cannot be tempted with evil, and he himself tempts no one. But each person is tempted when he is lured and enticed by his own desire. Then desire when it has conceived gives birth to sin, and sin when it is fully grown brings forth death.
James 1:13–15

34

UNPLUG FROM OUTRAGE GENERATORS

During Q&A at a luncheon in Owensboro I was headlining, an attendee shared his view that the country had no hope as long as Obama was president. He was adamant and angry. He asked what news sources he should plug into for reliable analysis. My advice was to stay away from inflammatory news outlets that specialized in giving more heat than light, outlets whose business model was to generate outrage to keep viewers glued to the set and sell advertising.

It's no surprise: if you spend hours every day plugged into an outrage generator, you will become outraged. If you listen to fearmongers, you will become fearful. If you're plugged into QAnon conspiracy theories, you will become suspicious. When we are filled with fear, suspicion, and outrage, our hearts have little room for love. More importantly, we will have lost our capacity to love. And indeed, it is love that will change lives and win over the culture.

Fear is not a Christian value. In his second letter to Timothy, Paul says, "For God has not given us a spirit of fear, but of power and of love and a sound mind" (2 Timothy 1:7 NJKV). Jesus consistently tells His people not to be afraid. It doesn't mean that we're never afraid, but it does mean that we identify the fear, give it over to Jesus, and, by His power, allow Him to work in us to overcome that fear. After all, He overcame the greatest fear by defeating the power of death and hell. Scripture tells us, "There is no fear in love, but perfect love casts out fear" (1 John 4:18).

Martin Luther King Jr. understood this as he led the civil rights movement in the 1950s and 60s. His strategy to win over the culture was based on biblical principles, and he spent much time encouraging and exhorting his followers to embrace those principles. In his book *Strength to Love*, King said, "Darkness cannot drive out darkness. Only light can do that. Hate cannot drive out hate. Only love can do that."[1]

If you find yourself prone to hate, consider what's causing it. If you're constantly afraid of the news or what the opposing political party is doing, stop clicking on all the doomsayers on social media. Stop tuning into the television and radio talk shows that peddle tribalistic enmity. Fear ends up producing hatred. And when we hate something, we want to crush it. This is opposite to Jesus's mission to redeem, restore, and renew the things that are broken.

When Jesus walked this earth, there was fear and suspicion all around. The Jewish people lost their place and power in the world. Their culture was deeply broken. Yet when Jesus looked at the culture of Jerusalem, he didn't fear it, condemn it, or call fire down from on high to consume it. When Jesus saw the culture, he had compassion, for "they were harassed and helpless, like sheep without a shepherd" (Matthew 9:36).

The only hope of the world is the church living out Christ's command to love. In 1966, Martin Luther King Jr. delivered a speech challenging his followers to a radical kind of love. He said, "Do to us what you will, and we will still love you. . . . throw us in jail, and we will still love you. Threaten our children, and bomb our churches and our homes and, as difficult as it is, we will still love you." Sounds impossible, but consider that violence didn't overturn Jim Crow. Radical love did. As the vicious racists bombed churches, trained firehoses on protestors, and beat and murdered their fellow image-bearers, love won the day.

Jesus emphasized love as the primary value of His kingdom: "By this, all people will know that you are my disciples, if you have love for one another" (John 13:35). If the church loses its ability to love, its mission is compromised and there is little hope for the world. If you want to change the world, go out and love the world. After all, God so loved the world, He gave His only Son as a sacrifice for it (John 3:16).

Reflection: What grid do you view our society through: compassion or fear? How do you view the role of leaders? Should they be dividers or builders? Have you considered the kind of media inputs you allow into your life? Have you noticed how they affect you? How can you improve your media diet?

For God has not given us a spirit of fear,
but of power, love, and a sound mind.
2 Timothy 1:7

35

DON'T WASTE TIME ON RUMORS

"I just heard that the county health department has several cases of Ebola, and they're trying to keep it a secret about what's going on." This was more bad news circulating during COVID shutdowns in the Commonwealth. In addition, we were in the middle of several projects needing our undivided attention. "So, how does this help me?" I responded quite directly to the colleague who brought this to my attention. "Why do I need to know this right now?" I was firm, but it needed to be asked. There was serious work to be done; spending any amount of time chasing down rumors irrelevant to the tasks at hand seemed like a waste of time.

I get it. People want to be in the know, and they want to be the first to convey what they believe to be important information. This is a very real human trait. But in the world of politics, it's essential to prioritize the issues, budget your time, and focus on the most important things. To achieve your organization's goals, you must use your time wisely to complete the tasks that further your organization's goals. Anything outside of your goals, tasks, and issues is a distraction. I call these distractions political alligators. They have big mouths, take a bite out of our time, and sap the energy needed to focus. We all have 24 hours in the day. The difference between the successful and the marginal in the public arena is how time is budgeted. Budgeting time wisely is the first step to productivity and effectiveness.

I was in my first month of serving on the Trigg County Fiscal Court when a longtime magistrate shared a list of the roads that would be paved. To my pleasant surprise, mine was one of them. Good news, right? Not exactly. The rumor on the street was that "Nelson ran only because he wanted his road to be paved." I had zero input in road projects. Zero. Yet, within days, the rumor mill was churning. I was later appointed to the transportation committee and eventually had significant input, rumors notwithstanding.

One need not serve in office to see that rumors fly fast, but it's worth noting that rumors start in many ways, including speculation, ignorance, or skullduggery. Noting the origin of a rumor helps determine how to address it. There might be a grain of truth somewhere in the rumor, but rumors are still rumors. They often start when participants in a discussion walk away with a different understanding or a different perspective. They might have missed some key points or seized on minor points and turned the story into something entirely different. It's easy to deviate from the facts by a few degrees. Sometimes rumors are built on conjecture; other times, they are simply meant to hurt. In any case, I eventually accepted rumors as the reality of the political world. To lighten up things, I adopted the maxim, "Believe nothing that you hear and only half of what you see." It's an exaggeration, but it has helped me cope with the rumors.

Indulge once again the political rumors as political alligators metaphor. Rumors can be exciting and dangerous, but rumors of any kind are something to avoid. They are time wasters and amount to nothing. If you fail to avoid the lure of the political alligators and the amusement they might bring, beware because they'll bite you every time.

Reflection: Do you know someone prone to talking about rumors? How can you steer them away from rumors next time they bring them up?

Have nothing to do with foolish, ignorant controversies;
you know that they breed quarrels.
2 Timothy 2:23

36

STAND ON PRINCIPLE, GO AGAINST THE GRAIN

I t was one of the first votes I took in 2011 as a magistrate on the Trigg County Fiscal Court. The county hospital was awarded a million-dollar grant to create a biofuel energy plant. Translation: if the hospital upgraded to using wood fuel for a heating source, the federal government would give it one million dollars. All that was required of the local government was to approve the measure.

Did anyone ask whether it was prudent and sustainable? Would it save the county money in the long run? What would a large smokestack do to the tranquil downtown area? What about wood trucks coming into town on a regular basis? During the discussion, I was told it was "free money"—no strings attached. This didn't sit well with me. "But this is somebody's money," I responded. "It's the taxpayers' money." I wasn't convinced it was a good use of funds, and I was the only magistrate to vote no to the "free money."

President Barack Obama pushed a nearly trillion-dollar stimulus package through Congress in 2009. It became clear that easy cash clouds clear thinking. Eventually, it was revealed that several multi-million-dollar projects scattered across numerous communities in America would be a bust.

One of the most difficult things in the political world is to say no to money from on high. There comes a time when political prudence tempered by fiscal responsibility says No. No to simple fixes with lots of zeros behind them. No to government shopping sprees and fulfilling "wish lists." No to saddling future generations with more debt.

Besides outright federal giveaways under the auspices of economic development, there are other ways that easy cash can cloud clear thinking. For decades, the horse racing lobby promised the state legislature hundreds of millions in annual revenue if only they'd legalize video slot machines. One year, they sent letters to local government officials showing how much of that revenue "windfall" could be used for roads, schools, and other infrastructure needs. It was bribery by discretion—using other people's losses as fodder for political persuasion. It was pathetic.

Good public policy protects citizens from predatory actors. It also provides a level playing field for all businesses. In principle, it opposes monopolistic practices and doesn't carve out special rights for an entire industry. In 2021, the Kentucky legislature welcomed into law a Trojan Horse of bad policy cloaked in cash when it approved Historical Horse Racing— essentially video slot machines. I'm convinced Kentucky's leaders were misled, and consequently, too many Kentuckians bad at math and prone to addiction will be deceived by the lure of quick cash. The bottom line is that quick and easy cash clouds clear thinking. Remember to always stand on principle. Go against the current, even when all others are swept away in the frenzied temptation of possible riches. Good leadership demands this.

Reflection: Have you considered how you might respond under public pressure? How can you prepare yourself to withstand public pressures and hold fast to your principles?

Forever, O Lord, your word is firmly fixed in the heavens. Your faithfulness endures to all generations; you have established the earth, and it stands fast. By your appointment they stand this day, for all things are your servants. If your law had not been my delight, I would have perished in my affliction.
Psalm 119:89–92

37

TEST OF CHARACTER: GIVE A MAN POWER

The phone conversation was tense. The candidate running for the state House seat in a Republican primary explained that the debate wasn't fair. It was on his opponent's home turf, and those in charge made sure to give his opponent every advantage. He was clearly upset, and it went downhill from there.

This was sad to witness, mostly because he should have known better as a follower of Jesus. His opponent, also a believer, went on to win the general election and is now an outspoken voice across the state for conservative values.

In a speech describing Abraham Lincoln's character qualities, Robert G. Ingersoll said, "Nothing discloses real character like the use of power. It is easy for the weak to be gentle. Most people can bear adversity. But if you wish to know what a man really is, give him power. This is the supreme test."[1] The testing of a political candidate begins on the campaign trail and ultimately reveals their character. The daily grind of meetings, messaging, and a myriad of attacks simply reveal what is already there.

Campaigning is a microcosm of how someone handles power. Pass the test, which, at a minimum, starts with some level of humility and grace, and the voters may reward the candidate with an opportunity to lead and govern. Fail the test by exuding arrogance, pride, and any hint to the voters that you'll misuse power, and victory is highly unlikely. Fall short on the basics—especially character—and victory on election day is unlikely.

Yet the standard of personal conduct is higher for those who identify as followers of Jesus. When candidates repeat ugly rumors and operate in haughtiness and rudeness, it reflects poorly on their character. Trials will surely come, and since we're human, we are bound to fail from time to time. However, if we make regular deposits of virtue into our souls, we're much more likely to weather the storms and trials wherever we are.

Reflection: What if the embittered political candidate mentioned above had attended the same church as his opponent? Would it have made a difference if they were neighbors? Have you considered how you'd treat a political opponent if you went to the same church? How about those outside the church?

Out of the abundance of the heart the mouth speaks.
Matthew 12:34

By this all people will know that you are my disciples,
if you have love for one another.
John 13:35

38

BEWARE OF FLATTERY

"Power tends to corrupt and absolute power corrupts absolutely."[1]

— LORD ACTON

Three things in large doses can undo a person: power, fame, and money. All three converge in politics. In order to get elected, it takes money to run a campaign. Once elected, power and fame come into play.

Power and fame go hand in hand with holding office. Lobbyists will curry favor with legislators, constantly making them feel important. They'll throw big receptions with fine food and important people in attendance. Flattery is common in the political world. It's easy for politicians to think more of themselves than they are. In the end, they're just regular people like you and me who happen to be entrusted with power.

The question is whether any political leader is capable of stewarding the position without being corrupted. Can they remain grounded and carefully guard themselves from such corruption? It's challenging yet possible. Surrounding yourself with trustworthy friends who will provide accountability is an important safeguard. A good spouse is really helpful. In my case, I'm involved with a men's group where we spend time in prayer and Scripture on a weekly basis. I've tried to build a level of accountability into my life, a safeguard to help keep me from going off the rails.

I was appointed to serve on the Trigg County Hospital Corporation Board, the entity that would decide the fate of the public hospital. The hospital was seeking approval for a $7 million loan to expand and build a surgical center. We were told that without a surgical center for outpatient surgery and the additional revenue it would generate, the hospital was doomed.

The board was split, and I held a pivotal vote. Leaders and influential community members made clear to me how important it was for the hospital to succeed. As a board member, the sudden importance of my role in the vote could have gone to my head. Being courted by the pillars of the community—the successful and the wise—can be heady. I've learned that it's a discipline not to conflate the importance of holding a position of leadership with self-importance. In other words, one must be grounded and tempered with humility.

Reflection: Do you have the character to withstand flattery? Have you endured pressure from people with influence and power? If not, how could you prepare to resist undue pressure in the future?

Keep your heart with all vigilance,
for from it flow the springs of life.
Proverbs 4:23

39

GOVERN CONSERVATIVELY

"Winning campaigns aren't always successful. And losing campaigns aren't always a failure." It took a few moments for this nugget to sink in to the attendees at CPC's inaugural training in 2013. Political consultant Mark Montini went on to explain that if you run as a conservative and get elected as a conservative but don't do conservative things once in office, you will not be successful. You will have failed to execute the goal of moving the political needle in a conservative policy direction. On the other hand, if you run a good campaign as a conservative and move your opponent to embrace conservative positions, and yet come up short, it is not a failure. You have successfully made a difference.

Getting elected is relatively easy. The hard part is governing. Will you hold to the values you campaigned on once you're in office? Don't ever forget your core principles. Don't ever forget who sent you to serve in office. Make sure to keep your promises and remember that power can easily go to your head. Be careful to temper it with the value of servanthood.

Keep in mind that you will leave office one day. Several years ago, two influential county-level politicians died in office very unexpectedly. Perhaps they considered what they were leaving behind, but one day, they woke up not realizing it would be their last day in their mortal bodies. Be sure to ask yourself what you're leaving behind.

You will also quickly discover that your vantage point radically changes once in office. Before, you were a citizen making the case that you should be elected. Now in office, you are in the seat of power, representing a diverse people with diverse allegiances. It has been said that governing is campaigning by different means. But in the end, it's really governing. Don't forget your core values and the people who voted you into office.

These are lessons I learned firsthand after being elected as Trigg County's 5th District Magistrate in 2010. It was humbling to be entrusted to represent voters in my district, and I looked forward to working with other county leaders to shape Trigg County's future. I had a zeal and earnestness to represent the county citizens well. After a few years in office, some of my preconceived notions of elected leaders changed. I was much more empathetic. I was more careful about speaking to the issues and how to enter the conversation. I believe that most Kentuckians would have a different attitude toward elected leaders if they served in office for even a short period of time.

With this said, I didn't budge on conservative principles. Montini's counsel was prescient. My election would be a failure if I failed to stand for conservative principles. I never voted for a tax increase and even voted against increasing the salaries and benefits of magistrates. I voted against a $1 million grant from the federal government because I thought it was wasteful spending. I worked behind the scenes with the county attorney and judge-executive to update the county's restrictions on sexually oriented businesses. And I angered a few constituents who wanted the county to gravel their private driveways, even though I was told that previous officials did it. Standing for your core principles is key, but growing to be effective in the job and responsibility of representing a diverse constituency takes maturity, something I'm still working on.

Reflection: Most people are not able to hold positions of leadership because, at the time of testing, they will waver. How do you think you'd fare under difficult trials? What makes you believe that?

~

But test everything; hold fast what is good.
Abstain from every form of evil.
1 Thessalonians 5:21–22

40

PROFILES IN LEADERSHIP

S ome of the greatest political leaders were the least likely leaders. Have you considered that Moses was inarticulate and didn't want the job that God called him to? Gideon was fearful, and David was underwhelming. None of them would have been chosen by their graduating classes to lead them in anything. Yet, they had one thing in common; they were called by God. The Creator of the universe put it on their hearts to lead His people.

Modern-day examples of leaders shaped by their Christian faith include William Wilberforce, who dedicated his political work to banning England's slave trade. William Carey pioneered educational opportunities for Indian women and campaigned against India's caste system and widow-burning. Abraham Kuyper gave a robust voice to Dutch Christians who wanted to shape politics, higher education, and the news media. Martin Luther King Jr., a pastor, led the American church to stand against Jim Crow and extend equal treatment under the law to black people.

There's a lot of talk about the failures and flaws of today's political leadership. It is the same kind of criticism anyone could have leveled at Moses—a murderer, David—an adulterer, or Gideon—an idolator. The truly amazing thing isn't that people fail miserably—it's that a just and holy God can use flawed human beings to do something great. As the old Gaelic saying goes, "God strikes straight blows with crooked sticks."

Lest you think leadership is only for certain people and not you, think again. Have you considered that you are likely a leader already? If you're a parent, a teacher, or an employer, you are leading whether or not you realize it. Others are watching and taking their cues from you. Have you considered how you're leading? For the follower of Jesus, love and servanthood are paramount to true leadership. Consider John Stott's statement: "The authority by which the Christian leader leads is not power but love, not force, but example, not coercion, but reasoned persuasion. Leaders have power, but power is safe, only in the hands of those who humble themselves to serve."[1]

The greatest leader in history, Jesus Christ, said that whoever will be first must be last (Mark 9:35), and he who is greatest in His kingdom must be a servant of all (Matthew 23:11). According to the world's standards, this is an upside-down way of leadership, but by embracing upside-down Kingdom principles, the world may once again be turned right side up.

Reflection: Have you considered Jesus's example of leadership? Do you think that integrating Jesus's principles into politics would change our culture for the better? If you're called to run for office, would you be willing to follow Jesus's model, even if it meant losing?

Trust in the Lord with all your heart, and do not lean on your own understanding. In all your ways acknowledge him, and he will make straight your paths.
Proverbs 3:5–6

Reflection: Have you considered there's a right time to speak and a right time to be silent? A right time to take action and a right time to be still? How do you discern when to act and when to speak?

Through patience a ruler can be persuaded,
and a gentle tongue can break a bone.
Proverbs 25:15 NIV

42

YOUR LIFE'S LEGACY

"Begin with the end in mind."[1] That's the main idea in Steven Covey's book *Seven Habits of Highly Effective People*. It's a good charge that we should think about often. Have you considered your legacy? As country music artist Randy Travis said, "It's not what you take when you leave this world behind. It's what you leave behind when you go."[2]

What are you doing with this great gift we call life? Are you stewarding it well? Are your actions pointing others to godliness? Are your policy positions reflective of eternal principles? Do the fruits of the Spirit accompany your mode of engagement? Is your tone inviting? Is what you're doing pointing to the One who called you?

Maybe it's not about *your* legacy. Whether serving in some great capacity in office or elsewhere, have you considered that there's a greater legacy? The Bible tells the story of a Creator who dared to humble Himself to become a servant. A King who would go to the cross to redeem you and me and all of His creation. A risen Savior who is in the process of restoring all that has been lost. In this great drama of redemption, God invites us to participate in a higher purpose, one much greater than accumulating entries on our résumé.

"Is what you're living for worth dying for?" the first-year college student asked the presidential scholar and basketball player while passing him in their dorm room hallway. "I notice that you're really smart, athletically talented, and have all the girlfriends. But is that all you were made for?" Those words dropped like a bombshell in my friend's soul as his fellow dorm resident casually walked away. The first question of the Westminster Shorter Catechism asks, "What is the chief end of man?" The answer is, "Man's chief end is to glorify God and enjoy him forever."[3] Anything less than that will amount to a disappointment in life, short of its highest purpose.

Sadly, there are many recent stories of our Christian leaders serving in powerful and influential positions that didn't end well. I'm reminded of Jesus's words: "For what shall it profit a man, if he shall gain the whole world, and lose his own soul?" (Mark 8:36 KJV). In your quest to make a difference in this world, give your life to the Living God. Jesus is the one writing your story. As He does so, glorify and praise Him in the process, even in the difficult times. *Especially in the difficult times.* And see what He will do in your life for His glory.

Reflection: Do you see public service as a ministry? Are you committed to allowing God to work through you? Is your goal to make the name of Jesus great?

For it is God who works in you to will and to act
in order to fulfill his good purpose.
Philippians 2:13

AFTERWORD

We got to the park a couple of hours before the others arrived. My wife Bobby Jo and I finally found a place on the Door Peninsula sheltered from the strong wind. The northerly gusts swept off the cool Green Bay waters and chilled the air. Less than 24 hours earlier, it was summer-like and in the 80s. But today, the thermometer struggled to push 70—typical Wisconsin weather in early September. We wanted to gather in one of my father's favorite places, near the water in Sturgeon Bay, blocks from where Dad grew up.

It was an impromptu family reunion with my dad's cousins and friends he grew up with in the area. We weren't even sure we'd be able to get together the day before since it depended on whether my dad had the strength to get out of the house. Less than three weeks earlier, he was diagnosed with stage 4 lung cancer. Two days before we gathered, he had completed his first round of chemotherapy. But there he was, propped up in a camp chair, feet resting on a cooler, soaking it in. He was quieter than usual and in some discomfort, yet you could tell he was happy to be surrounded by family and friends who loved him.

It was a bittersweet, sobering time for me and my family as we watched my father's health dramatically decline. A few weeks earlier, he was on the golf course with his buddies. The next morning, he was coughing up blood and sent to the emergency room. He was later diagnosed with cancer. It's part of life—sickness and disease, coping with bad news, and seeing your loved ones lose their health. Yet we modern people have been sheltered from the inevitable end of life called death, and we go to great lengths to avoid dealing with it.

My dad pulled some strings for my wife and me to stay at a close friend's cottage in Egg Harbor, immediately adjacent to the property of my grandparents' motel where my dad spent his summers. It was nostalgic for me to stay there, as it brought back memories from when I was a kid. His high school friend was very hospitable and generous to us. I couldn't help but notice the bumper sticker on her car parked in the drive. It said Equality for All. The small yard sign near the entrance said, "This home believes in science, tolerance, and equality"—all mantras of the political left. My dad told me we shouldn't talk politics because she was very far left on the political spectrum. Yet her hospitality, care, and compassion for my dad overshadowed any political differences at the moment.

Instead of a potential political enemy, I saw a person who cared deeply—doing what she could to help my dad. Even though our worldviews were vastly different, there was a certain part of our humanity we had in common. It's because we're made in the image of God that we're able to empathize, offer grace, and act with self-sacrifice. Common grace allows two human beings with vastly different beliefs to share the same care and compassion for a loved one.

The same God who created us in His image cuts through the external political differences and delves into issues of the heart. Jesus modeled humility and loved well. He came to restore the world and reconcile us to Him. He staked His life on this mission—literally. This is love. And it's through Christ that all things will someday be made new—even our politics.

ABOUT THE AUTHOR

Richard Nelson is the founder and executive director of the Commonwealth Policy Center. He's served on numerous boards, including the Kentucky Council on Postsecondary Education, Hopkinsville Community College Board (chair, 2020–2021), Kentucky Council on Environmental Education, Pennyrile Christian Community Board (chair, 2018–2021), Yes for Life Alliance, and Trigg County Hospital Corporation Board. Richard was elected to the Trigg County Fiscal Court as a magistrate in 2010 and served until 2014. He's an active member of Buck Run Baptist Church in Frankfort.

Richard's previous employment includes field biologist for the US Fish and Wildlife Service in Jamestown, North Dakota; research assistant in the Wisconsin State Capitol; policy analyst for the Family Research Institute of Wisconsin; and field representative and policy analyst with The Family Foundation. He earned a BS in biology, wildlife management, and resource management from the University of Wisconsin-Stevens Point in 1992 and a Master of Arts in public policy from Regent University in 1995.

He is certified by the Wildlife Society as a wildlife biologist and certified by the Wisconsin Department of Public Instruction as a secondary education teacher in environmental science.

Richard is an outdoors enthusiast and formerly ran an award-winning taxidermy studio in Cadiz, Kentucky. In his free time, he enjoys hunting, fishing, and camping. Father of three girls and a boy, he resides in Franklin County with his wife, Bobby Jo, on Dry Ridge Farm, a 39-acre working cattle farm in Bald Knob.

MORE PRAISE FOR CPC AND CHRISTIANITY & POLITICS

"I'm proud of my friend Richard for taking the time to share his wisdom on such a vital topic to Christians in our nation. For too long, apologists for the 'Christian left' have invested much time and energy telling biblical Christians that they can't be involved in politics and the public arena since we might somehow offend people. Richard believes, like I do, that we are the very people who don't want to offend anyone —we want to REACH them for the Lord! Richard handles this from a biblical perspective and walks us through the "Why" we must engage as well as the "How" we actually do that. Now IS the time for God's people to take a biblical stand, in love but unapologetic for telling the truth. . . . Richard tells us exactly what we need to do to make that happen!"

CHAD CONNELLY, former Republican National Committee Faith Outreach Director and Founder Faith Wins!

"Discover a compelling exploration of the intricate relationship between Christianity and politics in this thought-provoking book. Through insightful analysis and profound reflections, Nelson navigates the intersections of faith and governance, offering a nuanced perspective on how Christian values can and should inform and influence political decisions. This book is an essential read for anyone seeking to understand the role of religion in the public sphere and how faith can shape a just and moral society. It's a powerful testament to the enduring relevance of Christian principles in contemporary political discourse."

RILEY GAINES
12-time All-American swimmer, 5-time SEC champion at the University of Kentucky and Founder of The Riley Gaines Center at the Leadership Institute

"[This book] is an enjoyable and enlightening read, but most importantly, it provided one more example of what I have always said, 'If you want to make God laugh, just tell him your plans.' Richard discusses how God guided his life even if the direction he was sent wasn't always the path he thought he was going to take, nor the one he had planned for himself. This book provides good examples of how we must open our hearts fully to the course God has for us, and we should always be willing to surrender our lives to His will and His direction without exception. I encourage everyone to take the time to read this work, and I hope you find as much meaning in it as I did during my review."

MIKE HARMON
Former Kentucky Auditor of Public Accounts

"As someone who has been engaged in the public arena in various forms over the past two decades, I wish Richard had written this book a long time ago. I found his insight and counsel to be extremely inspiring, helpful, and an overall true 'how-to guide' of sorts on how to treat our fellow man through the eyes of Christ. I've long said it is ok to agree to disagree, but let's do it in a manner of love and humility. Richard takes those words to the next level, and his experience, biblical knowledge, and willingness to share his time-tested ways will prove inspiring and uplifting for everyone. I'm grateful he has taken the time to write this wonderful memoir and I know I will look to it often for guidance myself."

CHRIS GIRDLER

Former State Senator of Kentucky; President and CEO of Somerset-Pulaski Economic Development Authority

"Richard Nelson's *Christianity & Politics* expertly outlines how a unique but successful public policy organization can implement significant change in the public arena without being callous and arrogant.

Nelson's memoir is not just about politics—it is a common sense approach to dealing with people who share a different opinion than you do on social issues. The memoir is not just about politics—it details his spiritual journey and the personal trial of a failed marriage."

CHIP HUTCHESON

Former President of the National Newspaper Association

"Richard Nelson has created a masterful field guide to help Christians and concerned citizens grow in their understanding of how to be an active part of the political arena. *Christianity & Politics* will help guide you in practical ways for anyone wanting to take next steps for righteousness to prevail and advance. Also, this book could be used by small groups in any setting as a short-term curriculum for educational purposes. Enjoy the journey."

MARK HARRELL
Pastor of Victory Christian Church in Somerset, Kentucky

"I'm extremely honored to endorse Richard Nelson's new book about how God guided him to be a successful force to change the political landscape in Kentucky. This book will be an inspiration to thousands of conservative Christians in finding ways to bring the conservative message back as a strong force to America in a time when we desperately need it. We all can be agents of change, and Richard encourages us through his walk to really see what can be done."

ARNI JACOBSON
Chairman of Wisconsin Faith and Freedom
Former Green Bay Packer Chaplain

"*Christianity & Politics* details how Richard Nelson became a powerful influencer in Kentucky's public policy debate and how you, too, can make a difference by engaging. It is an encouraging read for those engaged or thinking of engaging in public policy."

ROBBY MILLS
State Senator and 2023 candidate for Lt. Governor

"This significant work is timely and important. It will encourage and challenge Christians and those who have not accepted Christ. Having known Richard for years and having seen him work, pray, succeed, deal with rejection and setbacks, and continue to persevere is impressive. I know his heart and discernment. I am proud to be brothers in Christ with him and I am enthused about the impact this book will have on humanity. I believe it is a must-read for current and future generations."

STEVE KECK
Founder, 5 Talents Financial and Somerset Recycling

"I am delighted that my friend Richard Nelson has captured both his experience and his passion in a book offering wisdom to Christians in the public arena. As one who has served in elected office, I can affirm that committed Christians are both a minority and a critically needed influence in that sphere. Richard offers insight and encouragement to those who are called to take up that cross and follow where Christ leads them. If you are one of those who are called and chosen (Matthew 22:14), you should read and heed the counsel offered in this book."

RET. AIR FORCE COLONEL TIM MOORE
Kentucky State Representative, 2007–2019; Founder, the Pro-Life Caucus and the Prayer Caucus in the Kentucky Legislature; Senior Evangelist, Lamb & Lion Ministries

"This is a very refreshing read. Richard Nelson writes about his wandering away from the Christian faith while in college and re-embracing it in his 20s. He describes the development of the Commonwealth Policy Center and its goal of encouraging candidates with biblical values to seek political office. He emphasizes that discussing issues with those who differ should never be done in an antagonistic or hateful manner, but should exhibit respect, civility, and, frankly, love and compassion as exhibited by Christ. He points out his conviction that the state should never be able to dictate religious or doctrinal positions of one faith group or another, but must support matters of morality. He deals with the challenges he has faced in his work and an extremely painful disappointment he faced in his personal life, which Jesus' love carried him through. Conservatives, for the most part, will approve of this memoir, but those on the other side of the political fence may find that though Nelson may not have converted them to his point of view, they may surprisingly gain a deeper understanding and possibly even appreciation of his winsome advocacy of conservative Christian principles. Time reading this book will be well spent."

DON NEAGLE
Member of the Kentucky Broadcasters Hall of Fame
and WRUS radio show host

"[This] book is both informative and encouraging. This will be insightful and helpful to those hoping to serve in a political way but also for those who want to walk in the steps of Jesus! I made many notes from beginning to end."

DAWN REED
Writer and Contributor to Kentucky Today

More Praise for CPC and Christianity & Politics

"Navigating the waters of public policy as a Christian without surrendering our convictions is difficult work. Thankfully, Richard Nelson's book *Christianity & Politics* provides an easy-to-read guide on thinking through difficult issues. More than a book about social and political issues, Nelson shares his own story. This unique approach keeps the reader's attention and guides us to a clearer application of our faith in our beloved state."

KYLE MCDANNELL
Executive Director, Capitol Commission

"In *Christianity & Politics*, Richard provides a storehouse of wisdom and instruction for those seeking to extend godly influence into the public arena. Written by an experienced cultural contender, this book will encourage you, fill you with hope, and will accurately guide you into cultural engagement with confidence and skill. Works of this kind are few and far between. I wholeheartedly exhort you to take it up and give it a thorough reading! An odyssey awaits you in these pages, and at journey's end, you will find enlightenment and joy!"

KYLE REEDER
Pastor, The Solid Rock Baptist Church, Benton, Kentucky

"When I want to understand a public policy issue, or when I need someone to help me think through what should be the church's best and appropriate response, I immediately call the Commonwealth Policy Center for clearheaded, biblical counsel and answers. CPC has been a godsend to me and to Buck Run Baptist Church because Richard Nelson and his team have helped me survey the issues, consider the options, and allowed me to follow the path that was best for my congregation. They are completely aware of all the pertinent current issues that challenge the faith of Christian people, but they are even more saturated with the Word of God and equipped to help congregations and pastors see our contemporary world through the lens of God's timeless truth and unflinchingly see culture through that perspective. Pastors rarely have time to keep up with the lightning speed at which progressive issues threaten us or the conservative opportunities that sometimes present themselves. I am glad we have the CPC precisely for this reason, to help us weigh policies and movements we encounter today on God's eternal, biblical scale of divine justice."

HERSHAEL YORK, Dean of The School of Theology and Victor and Louise Lester Professor of Christian Preaching at The Southern Baptist Theological Seminary

NOTES

Introduction

1. C. S. Lewis, "Christian Apologetics," in *God in the Dock: Essays on Theology and Ethics*, ed. Walter Hooper (Grand Rapids: Eerdmans, 1970), 101.

4. God Calls

1. Frederick Buechner, *Wishful Thinking: A Seeker's ABC*, rev. and exp. ed. (San Francisco: HarperOne, 1993), 119.

5. Begin in Prayer

1. Elisabeth Elliot, "Women: The Road Ahead," *Elisabeth Elliot Newsletter* (March/April 1991): 3, https://cdn.elisabethelliot.org/newsletters/EE-News_1991_03_04.pdf.

7. The Importance of Vision

1. Grover G. Norquist, "The New Majority: The 'Leave Us Alone' Coalition, *Imprimis* 25, no. 5 (May 1996), https://imprimis.hillsdale.edu/the-new-majority-the-leave-us-alone-coalition/.

8. Loving Your Enemies Is Mandatory

1. Francis A. Schaeffer, *The God Who Is There* (Westmont, IL: InterVarsity Press, 1998), 54.

10. The Spiritual War behind Political Battles

1. "National opioid settlement finalized; Kentucy to receive $483 million," Kentucky Association of Counties, February 25, 2022, https://kaco.org/articles/national-opioid-settlement-finalized-kentucky-to-receive-483-million/.

11. Failure Doesn't Define You

1. Dan B. Allender, *Leading with a Limp: Take Full Advantage of Your Most Powerful Weakness* (New York: WaterBrook, 2006).

12. Growth within the Crucible of Political Attacks

1. Charles Spurgeon, *The Treasury of David*, vol. 5a, *Psalms 107–119* (New York: Funk & Wagnalls, 1886), s.v. Psalm 119:22.

14. Personal Brokenness, Public Shame

1. Martyn Lloyd-Jones, "General Consideration: A Sermon on Depression from Psalm 42:5," accessed June 5, 2024, https://www.mljtrust.org/sermons/spiritual-depression/general-consideration/.

15. God Works through Suffering

1. Gwen Kik and Teale Fackler, *Threads of Hope, Pieces of Joy: A Pregnancy Loss Bible Study* (N.p.: Benjamin Books, 1999).

16. Effectively Communicating in a Post-Truth World

1. Oxford Languages, "Word of the Year, 2016," Oxford University Press, November 16, 2016, https://languages.oup.com/word-of-the-year/2016/.

18. Do Your Words Condemn or Heal?

1. John Calvin, *Calvin's Commentaries: The Epistles of Paul the Apostle to the Romans and to the Thessalonians*, trans. Ross MacKenzie, Calvin's New Testament Commentaries, vol. 8 (Grand Rapids: Wm. B. Eerdmans, 1995), s.v. Romans 8:3 (p. 159).

23. Should Pastors Speak to Moral Issues?

1. Abraham Kuyper, "Sphere Sovereignty," in *On Charity & Justice*, ed. Jordan J. Ballor and Melvin Flikkema, trans. Harry Van Dyke, Abraham Kuyper Collected Works in Public Theology (Bellingham, WA: Lexham Press, 2022), 141.

24. Earthly Power and Ultimate Power

1. Mitch McConnell, *The Long Game: A Memoir* (New York: Sentinel, 2016), 254.

25. Should Pastors Endorse Political Candidates?

1. "Bevin urges politics at pulpit despite law," *The Courier-Journal*, October 4, 2016, https://www.courier-journal.com/story/news/politics/2016/10/04/matt-bevin-urges-politics-pulpit-despite-law/91569740/.
2. Paragraph (3) of subsection (c) within section 501 of Title 26 (Internal Revenue Code) of the U.S. Code (U.S.C.) describes organizations which may be exempt from U.S. Federal income tax.
3. George Washington, "Farewell Address," *American Daily Advertiser of Philadelphia*, September 19, 1796. An online copy of this address may be accessed through the Library of Congress at https://www.loc.gov/resource/mgw2.024/?sp=229&st=text.

26. When Pastors Become Partisan

1. Greg Locke, "Greg Locke Politics 'You Cannot Be a Christian and Vote Democrat,'" Torn Curtain by Joshua Simone, YouTube video, 0:59, https://youtu.be/W6LP2mg0NA0?si=gYLd89isotbqEf10.
2. Noah Bierman and Lisa Mascaro, "Donald Trump Supporter in South Carolina: 'We're voting with our middle finger,'" *Los Angeles Times*, February 16, 2016, https://www.latimes.com/local/lanow/la-na-trump-south-carolina-20160216-story.html.

27. Six Objections to Christian Political Engagement

1. Gregory A. Boyd, *The Myth of a Christian Nation: How the Quest for Political Power Is Destroying the Church* (Grand Rapids: Zondervan, 2006).
2. "Dr. Martin Luther King, Jr. Speech at Illinois Wesleyan University, 1966," February 10, 1966, https://www.iwu.edu/mlk/.
3. Colin Kidd, "Civil Theology and Church Establishments in Revolutionary America," *Historical Journal* 42, no. 4 (December 1999): 1007–26, https://www.jstor.org/stable/3020934.
4. United States Library of Congress, "Jefferson's Letter to the Danbury Baptists: The Draft and Recently Discovered Text, *Information Bulletin* 57, no. 6 (June 1998). https://www.loc.gov/loc/lcib/9806/danpost.html.

5. Lord John Fletcher Moulton, "Laws and Manners," *Atlantic Monthly* 134 (July 1924): 1.

6. John Adams, "Letter from John Adams to Massachusetts Militia," October 11, 1798, in *The Works of John Adams, Second President of the United States: with a Life of the Author, Notes and Illustrations, by his Grandson Charles Francis Adams*, vol. 9 (Boston: Little, Brown, 1854), https://oll.libertyfund.org/titles/adams-the-works-of-john-adams-vol-9-letters-and-state-papers-1799-1811#lf1431-09_head_222.

7. Friedrich Nietzsche, *Human, All Too Human: A Book for Free Spirits*, pt. 1, trans. Helen Zimmern (Edinburg: T. N. Foulis, 1920), 15.

8. At the time of this writing, seven states (Arkansas, Maryland, Mississippi, North Carolina, South Carolina, Tennessee and Texas) still have laws on their books, although unenforceable, restricting atheists from holding office.

9. Benjamin Franklin, speech, "Thursday June 18th in Convention," in *The Debates in the Federal Convention of 1787, Which Framed the Constitution of the United States, Reported by James Madison, a Delegate from the State of Virginia*, ed. Gaillard Hund and James Brown Scott (New York: Oxford University Press, 1920), 181.

31. Understand the Political Landscape

1. John Archibald Wheeler, "The Outsider," *Newsweek* 93, no. 11 (March 1979): 67.

33. Avoid Negative Influences

1. Joe Gerth, "Jeff Hoover, other legislators have turned state Capitol into sleazy pickup joint," *The Courier-Journal*, November 5, 2017, https://www.courier-journal.com/story/news/local/joseph-gerth/2017/11/05/jeff-hoover-sexual-harassment-kentucky-capitol-culture-sleazy-gerth/833698001/.

2. John Cheves, "Attorney: Kentucky Legislature Paying $400,000 to Settle Sexual Harassment Lawsuits, *Lexington Herald Leader*, July 33, 2015, https://www.kentucky.com/news/politics-government/article44611674.html.

3. WUKY, "Jeff Hoover Resigns Leadership Post after Texts with Staffer," November 5, 2017, https://www.wuky.org/local-regional-news/2017-11-05/kentucky-house-speaker-jeff-hoover-resigns-leadership-post-after-texts-with-staffer

34. Unplug from Outrage Generators

1. Martin Luther King Jr., *Strength to Love* (New York: Harper & Row, 1963), 45.

37. Test of Character: Give a Man Power

1. Robert G. Ingersoll, "Ingersoll on Lincoln," *Ann Arbor Courier*, February 16, 1883, https://aadl.org/node/171839.

38. Beware of Flattery

1. Lord Acton to Bishop Creighton, "Letter I," in Acton-Creighton Correspondence, April 5, 1887, https://oll.libertyfund.org/titles/acton-acton-creighton-correspondence#.

40. Profiles in Leadership

1. John R. W. Stott, *Involvement*, vol. 2, *Social and Sexual Relationships in the Modern World* (New York: Fleming Revell, 1985), 259.

41. Spending Political Capital

1. The text of Kentucky Constitutional Amendment 2 (House Bill 91) is available at https://apps.legislature.ky.gov/law/acts/21RS/documents/0174.pdf.
2. Dobbs v. Jackson Women's Health Organization, 597 U.S. 215 (2022).

42. Your Life's Legacy

1. Stephen R. Covey, "Habit 2: Begin with the End in Mind," in *The 7 Habits of Highly Effective People: Powerful Lessons in Personal Change*, 30th anniversary ed. (New York: Simon & Schuster, 2020), 109–66.
2. Randy Travis, "Three Wooden Crosses," YouTube video, 3:21, https://youtu.be/UiDjPR9yRDU?si=1cDyvMFLXeeQSuzR.
3. Westminster Divines, *The Westminster Shorter Catechism with Scripture Proofs* (Edinburgh: Banner of Truth Trust, 2010), 5.

Made in the USA
Columbia, SC
28 September 2024